FROM CAIRO TO WALL STREET

FROM CAIRO TO WALL STREET

VOICES FROM THE GLOBAL SPRING

EDITED BY

ANYA SCHIFFRIN AND

EAMON KIRCHER-ALLEN

FOREWORD BY

JEFFREY D. SACHS

INTRODUCTION BY

JOSEPH E. STIGLITZ

20 YEARS

THE NEW PRESS

© 2012 by Anya Schiffrin and Eamon Kircher-Allen
Foreword © 2012 by Jeffrey D. Sachs
Introduction © 2012 by Joseph E. Stiglitz
All rights reserved.
No part of this book may be reproduced, in any form, without written permission from the publisher.

Requests for permission to reproduce selections from this book should be mailed to Permissions Department, The New Press, 38 Greene Street, New York, NY 10013.

Published in the United States by The New Press, New York, 2012
Distributed by Perseus Distribution

ISBN 978-1-59558-827-2 (pbk.)
CIP data is available

Now in its twentieth year, The New Press publishes books that promote and enrich public discussion and understanding of the issues vital to our democracy and to a more equitable world. These books are made possible by the enthusiasm of our readers; the support of a committed group of donors, large and small; the collaboration of our many partners in the independent media and the not-for-profit sector; booksellers, who often hand-sell New Press books; librarians; and above all by our authors.

www.thenewpress.com

Book design and composition by Bookbright
This book was set in Adobe Garamond

Printed in the United States of America

10 9 8 7 6 5 4 3 2 1

For our parents

CONTENTS

FOREWORD
THE GLOBAL NEW PROGRESSIVE MOVEMENT

December 2, 2011—Around the world, young people—students, workers, and the unemployed—are bringing their grievances to the public square. Protests have spread throughout the world, from Tunis to Cairo, Tel Aviv to Santiago de Chile, and Wall Street to Oakland, California. The specific grievances differ across the countries, yet the animating demands are the same: democracy and economic justice.

Many factors underlie the ongoing global upheavals. Protests in North Africa at the start of 2011 were fueled by decades of corrupt and authoritarian rule, increasingly literate and digitally connected societies, and skyrocketing world food prices. To top it off, throughout the Middle East (as well as Sub-Saharan Africa and most of South Asia), rapid population growth is fueling enormous demographic pressures. The protests spread from North Africa worldwide. Everywhere the fundamental concerns have been the same—political representation and the growing gaps between rich and poor—but local circumstances have of course differed.

The demographic challenge stands out in the North African protests. Egypt's population, for example, more than doubled over the course of Hosni Mubarak's rule, from 42 million in 1980 to 85 million in 2010. This surge is all the more remarkable given that Egypt is a desert country, with its inhabitants packed along the Nile. With no room to spread out, population densities are rising to the breaking point. Cairo has become a sprawling region of some 20 million people living cheek-by-jowl, with inadequate infrastructure.

Rapid population growth means a bulging youth population. Indeed, half of Egypt's population is under age twenty-five. Egypt, like dozens of countries around the world, is facing the extreme, and largely unmet, challenge of ensuring productive and gainful employment for its young people.

Employment growth is simply not keeping up with this population surge, at least not in the sense of decent jobs with decent wages. The unemployment rate for young people (i.e., those fifteen to twenty-four years old) in North Africa and the Middle East is 30 percent or more. The frustration of unemployed and underemployed youth is now spilling over into the streets.

Yet the problem of high youth unemployment is certainly not confined to the developing world. In the United States, the overall unemployment rate is around 9 percent, but among eighteen- to twenty-five-year-olds, it is a staggering 19 percent. And this number includes only the young people actually at work or looking for work. Many more have simply become discouraged and dropped out of the labor force entirely: not at school, not at work, and not looking for work. They don't protest much, but an astounding number end up in prison.

The problem of youth unemployment reflects much larger and deeper problems of inequality of income, education, and power, problems that are common throughout the world. The young people occupying Wall Street and protesting in hundreds of American cities are channeling sentiments felt very widely throughout American society. Their defining message, "We are the 99 percent," draws attention to the way that the rich at the very top have run away with the prize in recent years, gaining great wealth and great political sway while leaving the rest of society to wallow in wage cuts, unemployment, foreclosures, unaffordable tuition and health bills, and for the unluckiest, outright poverty.

It's not just the vast wealth at the top that they are questioning, but how that wealth was earned and how it's being used to twist politics and the law. Around 1980, the forces of globalization began to create a worldwide marketplace connected by finance, production, and technology. With globalization came new opportunities for vast wealth accumulation. Those with higher education and financial capital have generally prospered; those without higher education and financial capital have found themselves facing much tougher job competition with lower-paid workers halfway around the world.

Yet inequality of income has also led to inequality of political power, leading to governments that simply don't care enough about the working class and poor to make the needed investments on behalf of the broader society. We have a vicious circle instead. The rich get richer and also more powerful politically. They use their political power to cut taxes and to slash government services (like quality education) for the rest of society. Wealth begets power, and power begets even more wealth.

The world's labor markets are now interconnected. Young people in countries as diverse as Egypt and the United States are in effect competing with young Chinese and Indian people for jobs. China's low-paid, reasonably productive manufacturing workers and high-quality infrastructure (e.g., roads, power, ports, and communications) have set the standard for competitiveness globally. As a result, low-skilled workers in Egypt, the United States, and other countries must either raise their productivity enough to compete at a decent wage or accept extremely low pay or outright unemployment.

So creating decent jobs at decent wages is at the heart of being internationally competitive. That competitiveness requires equipping young workers with a good education, strong on-the-job training, and supportive infrastructure. While the private sector must create most of the jobs, the public sector must create the underlying conditions for high productivity. That is a tall order. It requires decent government, trying to help the many, not just the few. It requires governments that collect enough tax revenues to be able to afford education, job training, technology, and infrastructure investments.

Only one high-income region has done a reasonably good job of avoiding the wealth–power spiral, and therefore a good job of preparing its youth and its overall economy for tough global competition: Northern Europe, including Germany and Scandinavia (Denmark, Finland, Norway, and Sweden). In these countries, public education is at a high standard and the transition from school to work often involves programs like the apprenticeships for which Germany is especially famous. In other countries, notably including the United States, politics have amplified the surge in wealth of the new financial elite, and political financial elites have used that power to cut their own taxes rather than to invest in the education and skills of the broader society.

In developing countries, too, governments that emphasize excellence in education, public investment in infrastructure, and serious on-the-job training are the ones making the biggest economic and social advances. South Korea is probably the leading success story, with its superb educational attainment and strong employment of young people having taken it from developing-country status to high-income status within one generation. And South Korea has accomplished this feat in China's intensely competitive immediate neighborhood.

The United States, alas, is a case of massive political failure. American society has everything imaginable: a huge, productive economy, vast natural resources, and a solid technological and educational base. Yet it is squandering these advantages because the rich have lost their sense of responsibility and are far more interested in their next yacht or private plane than in paying the price of civilization through honest and responsible taxation and investment. The result is an American society that is increasingly divided between rich and poor, with shrinking social mobility between the classes.

American children raised in affluence succeed in obtaining an excellent education and have good job prospects after a bachelor's degree. But, as the rich have successfully pressed for tax cuts and reductions in government spending, children from poor and working-class households are far less likely to receive a high-quality education, and the U.S. government has failed to provide for training or adequate infrastructure. The result is a growing youth unemployment crisis among poor and working-class youth.

Vast inequality of income, combined with the sense of injustice and the loss of democratic accountability of the rich, explains why the protests have exploded not only in economies in crisis, but also in Chile and Israel, two countries doing well in economic growth and employment. Chile and Israel, together with the United States, have among the most unequal economies in the high-income world. As in the United States, a small proportion of households in both Chile and Israel hold an enormous proportion of the wealth.

Protests come to the streets when the normal political channels are blocked. In Tunisia and Egypt, the blockage was the most severe: long-standing authoritarian rulers and their families kept a tight grip on power (with the foreign policy support of the United States, it should be mentioned). In the United States the blockage is vastly more remediable but is insidious nonetheless. Americans elected a president in 2008 who promised change, but since the president and Congress fund their campaigns from Wall Street, Big Oil, and the health insurance industry, the change has been underwhelming. The Occupy movement in the United States exists because the U.S. government responds far more to powerful lobbies and interest groups than to the poor and middle class. Recent studies have shown that members of Congress are also engaged in substantial insider trading of stocks. In other words, they are dealing with corporate lobbies not only to fund their campaigns but also for immediate self-enrichment.

The political power of the rich has also led to an environment of impunity in which the rich feel that they can break the law and get away with it. In the United States, this feeling has been nowhere more evident than on Wall Street itself. The marquee Wall Street companies—Goldman Sachs, Citigroup, JP Morgan, and others—not only gambled recklessly with other people's money but also crossed the line into financial fraud. These financial houses teamed up with hedge funds to package toxic assets to sell to unwitting investors so that the hedge funds could bet against these toxic assets while the banks took home large fees and bonuses. This kind of behavior contributed to the financial crash that has devastated much of the world economy, yet those responsible for these misdeeds have generally gotten away with it, aside, perhaps, from a mild slap on the wrist. The Occupy movement is therefore also about the return to accountability and a rule of law.

If the worldwide protests have focused on four targets—extreme inequality of wealth and income, the impunity of the rich, the corruption of government, and the collapse of public services—then the future of the protest movement also involves four types of actions. The first is social activism to raise public awareness of the threats to society from the massive inequality of wealth and power. That begun in 2011 thanks to the youth protests around the world. The second is activism to bring key economic sectors under more democratic control. Consumer boycotts, shareholder activism, and student organizers can play a role in mobilizing actions to restore democracy from the hands of unaccountable corporations and the wealthy. The third is an affirmative view of politics in which government once again takes on the challenges of quality education, science, technology, job training, environmental protection, and modern infrastructure.

The fourth is the struggle for political power itself, in which candidates for the poor and middle class will have to win elections over the representatives of the rich and well-connected elites. This may seem like an impossible task. Money speaks with a loud voice in politics. Campaigning typically relies on expensive advertising and large spending. Yet my theory is that in the age of social networking—Facebook, Twitter, YouTube, and more—it will be possible to run effective campaigns on the energies of committed people, without vast sums. In other words, in the new network age, commitment and truth can outpace money and greed.

Young people around the world are setting the globe on a new path. A new generation of leaders is just getting started. The New Progressive Movement has begun.

Jeffrey D. Sachs

PREFACE
WHAT TOOK US SO LONG?

When the global financial crisis started with the collapse of the subprime mortgage market in the spring of 2007, it became clear that the world economy was facing a severe downturn and that unemployment would rise. At that time, my husband remarked that there would likely be protests all over the world. For the last few years we wondered about why there wasn't more outrage, and we speculated about where the first protests would take place. But we did not expect that we would be in Cairo just a few days before the historic events in Tahrir Square.

On January 14, 2011, we went to dinner in Cairo with a group of academics, alumni, and business people organized by Nagla Rizak and Lisa Anderson from the American University of Cairo. As the meal began, Anderson approached the podium and announced that Ben Ali had just left Tunisia. Immediately, the room broke out into cheers and people started clapping and chanting, "Us next. Us next." The people at our table whipped out their cell phones and began calling their friends in Tunis. The following day we went to lunch with some Egyptian government officials, and their nervousness was palpable. It was clear that something huge was beginning.

We flew on to Europe and kept in touch with our friends in Cairo. They told us of the excitement in Tahrir Square. We followed

the disappearance of the police and the enthusiasm of the protesters, and we were heartened by how happy people were in Cairo.
We'd been in Tunisia in 2010 and had heard so many stories of the
corruption in the government and the intense disgust engendered
by the family of Ben Ali's wife, Leila Trabelsi. Now it seemed that
change was in the air.

Like everyone, we spent the spring and then the summer watching the news and trying to keep up with the hectic pace of events:
Ben Ali leaving Tunisia, Mubarak falling, and the spread of protests to Syria, Bahrain, Libya, and Yemen. We have many friends in
Greece and so we heard constant accounts of the pressure that austerity was putting on the lives of the people there, and how the collapse of the Greek economy, the budget cuts and shrinking wages
were hurting so many. We went back to Tunisia in May 2011 and
heard our friends describe how life had changed. Mixed with the
uncertainty of the political situation was great excitement about
what was to come and an affirmation of the power of the people.

On a second trip to Egypt in July 2011, we had the privilege of
spending time with Jawad Nabulsi and his colleagues, commonly
referred to as *The Youth*. They told us how they had planned the
protests, described the scenes in Tahrir Square, and spoke of their
hopes for Egypt, the development projects they were planning, and
their expectations that democracy would prevail. Strangers told us
there was a new atmosphere of dignity and pride in the streets.

Not everyone was optimistic. In Alexandria we met Coptic
Christians who were afraid of a new intolerance. Patience had also
run out for the military. "It's time for them to leave," an old friend
told me, echoing what so many said to us. The economy was in a
mess, with tourism falling, unemployment high, and politics preventing the government from accepting foreign aid that was needed
to build housing and infrastructure. In Athens in July, we saw the
protests in Syntagma Square, already waning as an unusual heat
wave descended over the city, with temperatures topping 100 de-
grees. We heard over and over again how hard life had become and

how few options were available as the European Union demanded savage cuts in return for financial support to the government.

We then spent a few days in Madrid. The 15M protesters, who took their name from the date on which their protest began (May 15) and who had originally gathered in the Puerta del Sol, had returned for another gathering in July, bringing together protesters from around the country. We saw the protesters each day, attended a rally in front of the train station, and enjoyed the witty signs and slogans. To the flutter of hands, my husband spoke at a "teach in" on economics in Retiro Park.

Having spent time in Spain during the Franco regime, I was surprised by how respectful and good-natured the police were that week. In Madrid, people complained that the protesters didn't have clearly defined goals and dismissed them for being unfocused, but it was clear they were giving voice to the disgust and helplessness that people felt throughout the country. Youth unemployment was more than 40 percent, and nearly everyone we know was suffering from the crippling of the Spanish economy. The toll of the economic crisis was almost everywhere, and it seemed there was no end in sight. Governments had not done enough to protect people from the pain caused by the collapse of the mortgage market, the pressures on the euro, and the widespread joblessness and growing inequality. Instead, governments had been bailing out the banks, pushing austerity, and standing by while financial titans continued to take home large bonuses. The demonstrations in London in May against tuition hikes for students seemed like a sign of things to come, and as we traveled around Europe and the Middle East, we couldn't understand why we had not yet seen protests in the United States.

Then came Occupy Wall Street (OWS) and another wave of demonstrations around the world. It was amusing to see headlines proclaiming that the U.S. protests had spread across the globe. In fact, it felt that the United States had finally caught up with the rest of the world. The protests in America seemed small and tame compared to those in the other places we had been, but the demonstrations soon picked up momentum as well as press coverage. Some of the discussion was similar to what we heard in other countries—the feeling that the protesters didn't have a clear agenda, that they were naïve and disruptive. New York City Mayor Michael Bloomberg veered from grudging to downright hostile, but polls showed that New Yorkers were sympathetic to the cause as well as the legal right to demonstrate. Sadly, the police and local officials around the United States have not respected the right of assembly enshrined in our constitution. As my colleague from Columbia University Elazar Barkan points out, somehow in the discussion of the protests the question of free speech was lost, and the protests became the territory of city mayors, who framed it as a question of "don't step on the grass." As Barkan points out, "There is no reason to stop the protesters from staying as long as they want. They aren't doing any harm, and all the violence has been the police attacking the protesters, not the other way around." It was chilling to hear Mayor Bloomberg say in November, "I have my own army in the NYPD [New York Police Department], which is the seventh biggest army in the world."

We visited Zuccotti Park where the OWS protests were held and found the same spirit of commitment and enthusiasm and frustration and outrage that we had seen everywhere else in the world. The next morning I thought of a book that would tell the story of the global protests of 2011.

Gathering the essays in this book put us in touch with many people with a range of experiences. My co-editor, Eamon Kircher-Allen, and I spent time online trying to find people who could contribute. We spoke to many friends and acquaintances and wrote to some of the people who had contacted my husband after our visit with the *indignados* in Madrid. Finding contributors was not always easy. The demonstrators prided themselves on not having leaders, so it was often unclear who we should approach. In some parts of the Middle East, there was fear that contributing a piece would be dangerous. Some Arabs refused to appear in the book if it included an Israeli. And many of the most active protesters didn't have time to sit down and write, or weren't sure how best to tell their stories. Many were uncomfortable writing about themselves. They preferred to focus on the causes they fight for. Others don't speak English, so we offered editing and translation help. Some were in hiding. One woman in Bahrain even offered to smuggle a letter from her husband out of the prison where he is being held.

The voices in this book are not definitive or comprehensive. It's impossible for a handful of essays to sum up the rich diversity of the protests of 2011. But despite the differences in nationality, similarities in experiences were apparent. The problems of foreclosures and joblessness, the struggle against police brutality, inequality, and government austerity came up again and again. The reliance on social media, including Facebook, was a recurring theme. The use of General Assemblies to make group decisions and the feeling of community in the protests and the encampments are notable. So many protesters felt they were part of a larger wave of discontent and that they were finally heard. They didn't always have clearly defined political views, but they took to the streets because of frustration and a feeling that it was time to express their belief in the power of ordinary people to hold government to account. What's clear is how emotional the experience was and how much the protesters around the world enjoyed the feeling of connectedness. The essays from *indignados* from Greece and Spain describe the pleasure of getting to know other people and hearing their stories. Sitting in the squares of their home cities, they say they spoke to their neighbors for the first time. Other protesters got that same feeling from social media. Facebook connected them to like-minded people in their neighborhoods, cities, and countries and around the world.

Of course, it is easy to assume everyone agrees with you when you are online with like-minded individuals. Perhaps it becomes easy to forget that that not everyone agrees with you. The tear gas and the beatings—described in so many of the essays—reminded the protesters that they faced opposition, but they were heartened by the knowledge that they were not alone, that others faced the same economic problems and felt the same feelings of outrage and indignation. The protesters looked at Tunisia and Egypt and Spain and felt empowered.

The inspiration of Tahrir Square infused many of the essays we received and so did the hope that the events of 2011 had truly changed the world. Many of the protesters are optimistic and determined, but some are perplexed and don't understand why governments have not responded to the problems they outline in such detail. We don't have many answers in this book, but I hope that these essays will at least begin to explain why there is so much anger and frustration and how it surfaced in 2011. If nothing else, the voices of these courageous and civic-minded individuals will convey the spirit that is behind so much of the unrest.

How thousands of activists will be able to shape the future of their countries is uncertain. In Tunisia, the moderate Islamists won the last elections. In Egypt, the military is still firmly in control, and it looks like the country will resemble Chile after Pinochet where the military remained in control behind the scenes and was able to get seats in parliament and protection from the revised constitution. It's not clear if the protesters in Egypt will be able to run political parties that will bring about change. Nor is it clear whether the government has any interest in mobilizing The Youth's tech skills into e-government programs. Such programs could transform government finances by reducing corruption and boosting tax collection, providing funds to create jobs. I mentioned this to George Soros, and he noted that after the Czech revolution, many activists left politics and took on smaller projects based in their communities. That may be what happens in Egypt, too.

In Greece and Spain, hard times are ahead. The victory of the right-wing Partido Popular in Spain will bring about more austerity and cuts to spending, which will result in more unemployment and immiseration. In Greece, the government's hands are tied, and although there is disagreement about how to carry out austerity programs, the process has begun and will be painful. The Socialist government in Greece fell and in late November was voted out during elections. But their successors will find there is not much they can do to help the economy, and their failure will likely engender even more rage.

What the future will bring in the United States and United Kingdom is uncertain. In the United States, the OWS movements have managed to put the unhappiness about joblessness, income, and inequality consistently on the front page of the newspapers. In a short time, the OWS movement has changed the public debate. But will this success translate into protecting health care, spending on schools, expanding the social safety net, and passing a second stimulus package to help the economy? With the paralysis of the U.S. political system, it's doubtful. Indeed, leaders are unsure what anyone can do at this point to change economic policy in a meaningful way. It will be interesting to see how the protest leaders (for they do exist) will tackle these questions in 2012.

It may be that holding on to territory, whether it be parks or college campuses, is not ultimately going to have much effect on the political and economic power structures of the United States. Apart from public perception that these demonstrations are nuisances— dirty, disruptive, and dangerous—occupying physical space may prove to be a distraction from the task of organizing a sustained political movement that can be as effective as the union and student drive to get out the vote in the last U.S. presidential election. Re-creating that success will require discipline, organization, and the emergence of a strong leadership.

The physical geography of protest is relevant here. Tunisia and Tahrir Square overflowed into the streets and caused the collapse of two repressive regimes. For the OWS and Occupy London movements to have an impact on the political processes of the United

States and United Kingdom, they will also need to regroup over the coming months, become more centralized, and maybe even choose strong leaders in order to bring real and lasting change. This is the challenge of so many of the protests: how to go beyond the broad unhappiness with a broken system and help build a new one that is more fair, that protects the rights of minorities, and gives the 99 percenters more than just a voice but a real role to play in strengthening democracy.

Anya Schiffrin

ACKNOWLEDGMENTS

This book could not have been written without an extraordinary amount of support from people all over the world. Samantha Marshall did a superb job of editing many of the pieces, and Jane Folpe and Carmen de Paz Nieves worked with the Spanish contributors. We could not have included the Greek essays without the assistance of Apostolos Mangiriadis. Others who gave help and contacts include Mohammed Al Abdallah, Hannah Assadi, Amer Bisat, Julia Cunico, Sarah Gitlin, Dana Karnoush, Beth Kwon, Rob Johnson, Akram Khelifa, Laura Litunya, Charles Marshall, Matteen Mokalla, Nelson Montanino, Mustapha Nabli, Isabel Ortiz, Nagla Rizak, Francisca Skolnick, and Matt Stoller.

Finally, we thank The New Press and the contributors for agreeing to be a part of this project.

INTRODUCTION
THE WORLD WAKES

Joseph E. Stiglitz

There are times in history when people all over the world seem to rise up, to say that something is wrong and to ask for change. This was true of the tumultuous years of 1848 and 1968. It was certainly true in 2011. In many countries there was anger and unhappiness about joblessness, income distribution, and inequality and a feeling that the system is unfair and even broken.

Both 1848 and 1968 came to signify the start of a new era. The year 2011 may also. The modern era of globalization also played a role. It helped the ferment and spread of ideas across borders. The youth uprising that began in Tunisia, a little country on the coast of North Africa, spread to nearby Egypt, then to other countries of the Middle East, to Spain and Greece, to the United Kingdom and to Wall Street, and to cities around the world. In some cases, the spark of protest seemed, at least temporarily, quenched. In others, though, small protests precipitated societal upheavals, taking down Egypt's Hosni Mubarak, Libya's Muammar Qaddafi, and other governments and government officials.

SOMETHING IS WRONG

Television, new technologies, and social media, mastered by the young, played an important role both in organizing the protests and in their rapid spread. Technology brought together vast numbers of people and, just as importantly, let them know that there was a way to express their unhappiness and anger. But underlying most of the protests were old grievances that took on new forms and a new urgency. There was a widespread feeling that something is wrong with our economic system, and the political system as well, because rather than correcting our economic system, it reinforced the failures. The gap between what our economic and political system is supposed to do—what we were told that it did do—and what it actually does became too large to be ignored. Governments around the world were not addressing the economic problems, and so the feeling of unfairness became a feeling of betrayal. Universal values of freedom and fairness had been sacrificed to the greed of a few.

That the young people would rise up in the dictatorships of Tunisia and Egypt was understandable. They had no opportunities to call for change through democratic processes. But electoral politics had also failed in Western democracies. There was increasing disillusionment with the political process. Youth participation in the 2010 U.S. election was telling: an unacceptably low voter turnout of 20 percent that was commensurate with the unacceptably high unemployment rate. President Barack Obama had promised "change we can believe in," but he had delivered economic policies that seemed like more of the same—designed and implemented by some of the same individuals who were the architects of the economic calamity. In countries like Tunisia and Egypt, the youth were tired of aging, sclerotic leaders who protected their own interests at the expense of the rest of society.

And yet, there were, in these youthful protesters of the Occupy Movement—joined by their parents, grandparents, and teachers— signs of hope. The protesters were not revolutionaries or anarchists. They were not trying to overthrow the system. They *still* had the belief that the electoral process *might* work, if only there was a strong enough voice from the street. The protesters took to the street in order to push the system to change, to remind governments that they are accountable to the people.

The name chosen by the young Spanish protesters—*los indignados*, the indignant or outraged—encapsulated the feelings across the world. They had much to be indignant about. In the United States, the slogan became "the 99 percent." The protesters who took this slogan echoed the title of an article I wrote for the magazine *Vanity Fair* in early 2011 that was titled "Of the 1%, for the 1%, and by the 1%."[1] The article cited studies that described the enormous increase in inequality in the United States—to the point where 1 percent of the population controls more than 40 percent of the wealth and garner for themselves more than 20 percent of all the income.[2] In other countries, the lack of opportunities and jobs and the feeling that ordinary people were excluded from the economic and political system caused the feeling of outrage. In his essay, Egyptian activist Jawad Nabulsi discusses how the system was fixed in favor of the upper classes, and he uses the word *fairness* repeatedly to describe what was lacking in Egypt under Mubarak.

America has often been a model for the rest of the world. And, unfortunately, the growing inequality in the United States is also found in most countries around the world.[3] Even more unfairly, in the United States and in some other countries, as economies have become more unequal, tax and expenditure policies have become less progressive; that is, the burden of taxation has been shifted from those who can best afford it to the rest of society, and basic social programs for the poor and middle class have been curtailed. The tax cuts for corporations and the rich that President George W. Bush heralded became the staple of reforms in many other countries at a time when there was a need for a move in the opposite direction.

Given the high level of youth unemployment around the world—30 percent in Tunisia,[4] nearly 45 percent in Spain, and 18 percent in the United States[5]—it was surprising that it took so long for the protest movements to begin. The unemployed included young people who had played by the rules, done everything that they were supposed to, studied hard and got good grades, but faced a stark choice: remaining unemployed or accepting a job far below that for which they were qualified. In many cases, there was not even a choice. There simply were no jobs and hadn't been for years.

Something else helped give force to the protests: a sense of unfairness. In Tunisia and Egypt and other parts of the Middle East, it wasn't just that jobs were hard to come by, but those jobs that were available went to the politically connected. In the United States, things seemed more fair, but only superficially so. People who graduated from the best schools with the best grades had a better chance at the good jobs. But the system was stacked because wealthy parents sent their children to the best kindergartens, grade schools, and high schools, and those students had a far better chance of getting into the elite universities. In many of these top schools, the majority of the student body is from the top quartile, while the third and fourth quartiles are very poorly represented.[6] To get good jobs, one needed experience; to get experience, one needed an internship; and to get a good internship, one needed both connections and the financial wherewithal to be able to get along without a source of income.

Around the world, the financial crisis unleashed a new sense of unfairness, or more accurately, a new realization that our economic system was unfair, a feeling that had been vaguely felt in the past but now could no longer be ignored. The system of rewards—who received high incomes and who received low—had always been questioned, and apologists for the inequality had provided arguments for why such inequality was inevitable, even perhaps desirable. The inequities had been growing slowly over time. It is sometimes said that watching changes in income inequality was like watching grass grow. Day by day, one couldn't see any change. But as those who live near abandoned subprime houses know all too well, within a few months, scrub and weeds can quickly replace the best of manicured lawns. Over time, the change is unmistakable, and so too, over time, the inequality has increased to the point where it cannot be ignored. And that's what's been happening in the United States and many other countries around the world.

Even in the United States, a country not given to class warfare, there is today a broad consensus that the top should be taxed at a higher rate or at least not taxed at a lower rate.[7] While some at the top may believe that they earned what they received through hard work, and it is their right to keep it, the reality (which many of the richest do realize) is that no one succeeds on his own. The poor often work far harder than the richest. In developing countries, the poor lack the chance of education and have no access to funds, and their economies are dysfunctional, but they work long hours carrying water, looking for fuel, and toiling at manual labor. Even in developed countries, life chances are affected by where one is born and the education and income of one's parents. Often it comes down to luck, being in the right place at the right time.

A sense of community should mean that those who have the good luck and are fortunate should share part of that with the less fortunate. That notion has been part of the social contract that has been the basis of civilization from time immemorial. And as societies have become richer and their structure has changed—with increased mobility and smaller families—more of the responsibility for fulfilling the social contract has been assumed by the state. Modern societies take into account that taxes may hurt incentives, and there is a never-ending debate about balancing the benefits and costs of taxation. We need to collect taxes from everyone, including the rich and business owners, but we want to make sure the tax code does not inhibit the growth of business and the jobs it creates.

Somehow, that sense of balance was lost in the years that marked the end of the last century and the beginning of this century, in the United States and in many other countries around the world. In the United States, taxes were reduced on the only group that had been doing well for the last quarter century. The lower taxes and weaker regulation were *supposed* to unleash powerful economic forces that would uplift everyone, but that promise didn't materialize. Republicans love to use a quote from former President John F. Kennedy that "a rising tide lifts all boats," and in that era, there was a grain of truth in that aphorism. But now, it is more accurate to say that the yachts with the tall masts rise but that the smaller boats are more likely to be wrecked on the rocks—and without life boats and life preservers, those in the little dinghies are likely to drown.

In this Great Recession, the United States and the world moved perilously toward—and over—the brink, into a crisis in which the only winners seemed to be those who created it. By the end of the first decade of the twenty-first century, most Americans were worse off than they had been at the beginning.

It was not just the worsening inequality that outraged the protesters of 2011. It was a sense that at least some of those incomes were not honestly earned. Injustice motivated the Occupy Wall Streeters just as it motivated the young Tunisians of the Arab Spring. If someone earns huge incomes as a result of a brilliant contribution that leads to huge increases in incomes of the rest of society, it might seem fair that he receive a fraction, perhaps a substantial fraction, of what he has contributed. Indeed, the dominant paradigm in economics attempted to justify societal inequalities by saying (I should say, *assuming*) that they were related to differences in "marginal" productivities: those who, at the margin, contributed more to society got more.

Now, in the aftermath of the crisis, it seemed grossly unfair that the bankers walked off with outsized bonuses while those who suffered from the crisis brought on by those bankers' reckless and predatory lending went without a job. It seemed grossly unfair that government bailed out the banks but seemed reluctant to even extend unemployment insurance for those who through no fault of their own could not get employment or to provide anything but token help to the millions who were losing their homes. What happened undermined the prevailing justification for inequality, that those who made greater contributions to society receive (and should receive) larger rewards. Bankers reaped large rewards even though their contribution to society—and even to their firms— had been *negative*. In other sectors, CEOs who ran their firms into the ground, causing losses for shareholders and workers alike, were rewarded with gargantuan bonuses. *[margin: Banks help growth though.]*

What happened in the midst of the crisis made clear that it was *not* contribution to society that determined relative pay but something else. The wealth given to the elites and to the bankers seemed to arise out of their ability and willingness to take advantage of others. It was unfair. *[margin: Purely negative? Really?]*

Politicians talked repeatedly about the importance of values. Among the most important values is fairness. Recent research in economics and psychology has shown the importance that individuals attach to fairness. But increasingly, Americans are coming to believe that their economic system is unfair—almost half in a recent poll.[8] Americans grasped that the Occupy Wall Street protesters were speaking to their values, which was why, while the numbers protesting may have seemed small, two thirds of Americans said that they supported the protesters. If there was any doubt of this support, the ability of the protesters to gather more than a hundred thousand signatures to keep their protests alive when New York Mayor Michael Bloomberg looked like he would shut down the camp at Zuccotti Park near Wall Street showed otherwise.[9] And this support was not just among the poor and the disaffected. At a performance of Brecht's *Three Penny Opera* at the Brooklyn Academy of Music, the audience mocked the bankers in the play at the line "It is better to steal from a bank than to found a bank." While the police may have been excessively rough with the protesters in Oakland—and the thirty thousand who joined the protests the next day seemed to think so—it was noteworthy that some of the police themselves expressed support for the protesters. *[margin: Who funds BAM?]*

Overseas, the essays in this book describe the support protesters received from passersby and local shopkeepers. In Egypt, people didn't need much urging to join the crowds in Tahrir Square. They poured in, following the protesters who marched there.

Fairness is not the only value that has become gradually undermined. America has always thought of itself as a land of opportunity, of *equal opportunity*. (In a sense, equality of opportunity is a basic aspect of societal fairness.) Horatio Alger stories of individuals who made it from the bottom to the top are part of American folklore. But increasingly, the American dream that saw the country as a land of opportunity began to seem just that: a dream, a myth reinforced by anecdotes and stories but not supported by the data. The chances of an American citizen making his way from the bottom to the top are less than those in most other advanced industrial countries, and they have decreased markedly in recent decades. *Is this true? How do I vet this claim?*

In a way, in America and throughout the world, the youthful protesters were taking what they heard from their parents and politicians at face value—just as America's youth forty years ago did. Then they scrutinized the values *equality*, *fairness*, and *justice* in the context of the nation's treatment of African Americans, and they found what was going on wanting. In 2011 they scrutinized the same values in terms of how our economic and judicial system works, and they found the system still wanting—and not just for African Americans but for poor and middle-class Americans of all backgrounds.

If President Obama and our court system had found those who had brought the economy to the brink of ruin guilty of some malfeasance, then perhaps it would have been possible to say that the system was functioning. Any system can be abused by malefactors, and ours had been. But in fact, those who should have been so convicted often were not charged, and when they were charged, they were found innocent (or at least they were not convicted). Evidently, it was permissible to engage in predatory lending, abusive credit card practices, risky lending, and speculation that could bring the economy to its knees, requiring massive bailouts. Hank Greenberg, the head of AIG when it embarked on the path that eventually led to a government bailout of more than $150 billion, was still feted by his fellow Wall Streeters and was never sent to prison. No charges were brought against Richard Fuld, chairman of financial firm Lehman Brothers, which was blamed for precipitating the global financial crisis. Lloyd Blankfein, the head of Goldman Sachs, which received massive injections of money from the government (both directly and indirectly, through AIG), was not charged with any malfeasance but rather was rewarded with a multimillion-dollar bonus. The Securities and Exchange Commission brought charges against Angelo Mozilo, head of Countrywide Financial, the country's most outrageous writer of subprime mortgages, but he was never convicted of any crime. In short, evidently, no one—neither individuals nor corporations—was held accountable. (A few in the hedge fund industry have been convicted subsequently of insider trading, but this is a sideshow, almost a distraction. The hedge fund industry did not cause the crisis. It was the banks. And it is the bankers who have gone, almost to a man, free.)

If no one is accountable, the problem must lie in the economic system. This is the inevitable conclusion and the reason that the protesters are right to be indignant. Every barrel has its rotten apples, but the problem, as MIT Professor Susan Silbey has written, comes when the whole barrel is rotten.[10]

A basic sense of values should, for instance, have made those who were engaged in predatory lending—imposing unfair and abusive loan practices on borrowers who lack financial sophistication—feel guilty. A basic sense of values should have made those who were lending to poor people beyond their ability to afford, with mortgages that were ticking time bombs—when interest rates increased, as they almost surely would, the poor would likely lose their homes and their life savings—feel guilty. A basic sense of values should have made those who were designing the credit card programs that led to excess charges for overdrafts in the billions of dollars feel guilty.

Almost all religions have inveighed against usury, and a basic sense of values should have meant that at least some of the bankers who were practicing usury—and fighting to make sure that the states did not restrict usury and predatory lending—should have felt guilty. But what is remarkable is how few seemed, and still seem, to feel guilty, how few were the whistle-blowers. Something has happened to our sense of values when the ends—making more money—justify the means, which in the U.S. subprime crisis meant exploiting the poorest and least educated.

Much of what has gone on can only be described by the words *moral deprivation*. Something *wrong* had happened to the moral compass of so many of the people working in the financial sector. When the norms of a society change in a way that so many have lost their moral compass—and the few whistle-blowers go unheeded—that says something significant about the society. The problem is not just the individuals who have lost their moral compass but society itself. Did the bankers do anything illegal?

What the protests tell us is that there was outrage and that outrage gives hope. Americans have always had an idealistic streak, reflected both in the instruction in schools and in political rhetoric. Kids read the Declaration of Independence, "all men are created equal," and they read the words literally, *all men*, white and black, and they believe them. They recite the Pledge of Allegiance, which promises "justice for all," and they believe it.

For older people, this homage to values may provide a way of partially addressing the cognitive dissonance created by a world that is so different from the values that are espoused. Those values may serve as long-term aspirations not to be attained in this world, to be striven for only so long as there doesn't have to be too much compromise with current comforts. But most young people have less stake in the current system and take these statements at face value. The world that they may inherit is as distant from the values that they were taught as the world that my generation was to inherit, in 1968, was from the values that were espoused then.

One response would be to stop talking about values. Rhetoric about equality, fairness, due process, and the like, the argument goes, don't have anything to do with how the world works. In politics, we would call this emphasis on reality over rhetoric *realpolitik*. What it amounts to is a kind of economic Darwinism. Let the system evolve and let the fittest survive. Our economic and social system has evolved over time, and there have been mutations. Most systems, like communism, are badly flawed, so let's let nature take its course. For now American-style capitalism is the best system.[11]

Such an argument (often unexpressed) sometimes seems to lie behind advocacy of American-style capitalism. There are, however, a number of problems with this perspective. At a theoretical level, this teleological perspective on evolution—that it leads to the best possible system—has no justification. Nor is it certain that a system that works now will have the resilience to meet future challenges.

It is precisely this inability to assess resilience that is one of the flaws of the modern market economy. America's economic system seemed to triumph for a while (despite its flaws), but the financial crisis showed that the market system wasn't resilient: the bankers had taken bets that, without government assistance, would have brought them and the entire economy down. But a closer look at the *system* showed that this was not an accident; the bankers had incentives to behave this way. The flaw was a systemic flaw.

That flaw might seem a relatively easy one to correct. Just align social returns and private incentives so that the bankers are motivated to act in the interests of society more broadly. Modern research in the design of incentive structures has explained how hard that is to do. There is always imperfect information. The banker knows more about the financial markets—the consequences of various actions he might take—than do those outside the sector. When things turn out badly for the rest of society, even if they turn out well for him, he can explain forcefully how he was doing what he thought was best for society; it was just bad luck that things turned out otherwise.

There is a second reason that aligning the interests of the bankers, for example, and the rest of society is so hard. Finance won't align their interests with those of the rest of society on their own, and they have enough power to stop others from doing it. The system works well for them. Why should they acquiesce to changes that would reduce their power? Attempts in the United States and Europe to create a safer and fairer financial system have repeatedly encountered political obstacles.

MARKET FAILURES

The scenario of the banker who justifies his selfish actions is but one example of the dissonance between what the youth had been told about our society and what they saw, a gap that could no longer be ignored. They had been told about the virtues of a market economy, and yet the market economy was not even delivering on the one thing that it seemed to be good at, growth and job creation. Rather, it was showing in an almost unprecedented way its weaker side.

The list of grievances against corporations was long, and longstanding. For instance, cigarette companies stealthily made their dangerous products more addictive, and even as they tried to persuade Americans that there was no scientific evidence of the dangers of their products, their files were filled with evidence to the contrary. Exxon had similarly used its money to try to persuade Americans that the evidence on global warming was weak, even though the National Academy of Sciences had joined with every other scientific body in saying that the evidence was strong. Chemical companies had poisoned the water, and when their plants blew up, they refused to take responsibility for the death and destruction that followed. Drug companies used their monopoly power to charge prices that were a multiple of their costs of production, condemning to death those who could not afford to pay.

The financial crisis itself had brought out more abuses. While the poor suffered from predatory lending practices, almost every American suffered from deceptive credit card practices. And while the economy was still reeling from the misdeeds of the financial sector, the BP oil spill showed another aspect of the recklessness: lack of care in drilling had endangered the environment and threatened jobs of thousands of people depending on fishing and tourism.

No one had ever claimed that the market would result in a fair, or even acceptable, distribution of income, only that it would produce more goods than any other system, and so, in principle, everybody *could* be made better off than in any alternative. Some economists even argued for "trickle-down economics." In short, the promise was that the benefits of growth would eventually be shared by all. Markets provided incentives to avoid waste. Demand would equal supply, and that meant that there would be jobs for anyone willing to work at the going wage.

If markets had actually delivered on these promises, then all of the sins of corporations, all the seeming social injustices—the insults to our environment, the exploitation of the poor—might have been forgiven. But the financial crisis raised questions about the capacity of the market economy to deliver on these promises. Indeed, the 2008 collapse of the global economy, originating from the United States, had undermined confidence in market capitalism and its seemingly most vibrant form, American-style capitalism.

But even before the crisis, the evidence was that the market economy was not delivering *for most Americans*. GDP was going up but most citizens were worse off. Not even the laws of economics long championed by the political right seemed to hold. Earlier, we explained how the theory that is supposed to relate rewards to social contributions had been falsified by the Great Recession. The theory holds that competition is supposed to be so strong in a perfectly efficient market that "excess" profits (returns in excess of

Is this a legit argument?

the normal return on capital) approach zero. Yet each year we saw the banks walking off with mega-profits so large that it is inconceivable that markets are really competitive. Standard courses in economics talk about the law of demand and supply, where prices are determined to equate the two. In the theoretical model, there is no such thing as unemployment, no such thing as credit rationing. But in fact, we have a world in which there are both huge unmet needs (e.g., investments to bring the poor out of poverty, to bring development to Africa and the other less developed countries in other continents around the world, to retrofit the global economy to face the challenges of global warming) and vast underutilized resources (e.g., workers and machines that are idle or not producing up to their potential). As of December 2011, some 25 million Americans who would like a full time job can't get one, and the numbers in Europe are similar.

In the United States, we are throwing millions of people out of their homes—as this book goes to press, some 7 million families have lost their homes since the financial crisis began, and another 4 million are expected to lose their homes. We have empty homes and homeless people.

Some people have said that we have a savings glut, but the problem is not that the world is saving too much, it is that our financial system—the same global financial system that brought on the crisis—failed to use the scarce savings in the best way. Rather than allocating capital to where there was a high social productivity, money went uphill—to the richest country of the world—rather than downhill, as it's supposed to go, from the rich to the poor. Hundreds of billions of dollars went to tax cuts for the rich. Hundreds of billions more went to fight wars that failed to enhance security, hundreds of billions more were spent on weapons that didn't work—against enemies that didn't exist; and still hundreds of billions more went to build houses that were beyond people's ability to afford.

Innovation and globalization provide the most recent—and the most important—contexts to observe the failings of the market.

Both were supposed to make our economy more prosperous, and yet both seem to have resulted in an economy in which most citizens are becoming worse off.

What I have seen happening in the United States is akin to what I saw as chief economist of the World Bank. Countries were told to strip away trade barriers that, it was said, kept people working in unproductive jobs. The wonders of the market would result in people moving from the low-productivity protected sector to, say, the high-productivity export sector. Yes, jobs would be lost, but the new jobs would be even better, and everyone would be better off. But what happened too often was different. The onslaught of cheap imports did lead to job destruction, as predicted, but the market did not create the promised new jobs. The result was that workers went from low-productivity protected sectors to zero-productivity unemployment.

In recent research, Bruce Greenwald and I have traced the roots of the Great Depression to an increase in agricultural productivity so rapid that fewer and fewer people were needed to grow the world's food. In the United States in 1900, a large portion of the labor force worked on farms; today less than 2 percent of the population grows more food than even an obese population can consume—and there are large amounts left over for exports. Over time, most people working in agriculture who were no longer needed looked for alternative employment. But at times, the movement away from agriculture was far from smooth. Between 1929 and 1932, agricultural prices plummeted, and incomes fell by an amount variously estimated at one-third or two-thirds. Such precipitous declines in income resulted in corresponding declines in demand for manufactured goods. Rural real estate prices plummeted and credit became unavailable, and so, despite their already low income, farmers were trapped in the declining sector. Just when migration out of the rural sector should have been increased, it came to a halt. If people had been able to relocate, if new jobs had been created, the increases in productivity would have been welfare-increasing, but

Where do these new jobs come from. The market cant provide thm so why do Joe

as it was, given the market failures, those in both the city and the rural sector suffered.

Today, Americans are losing jobs in manufacturing largely because productivity increases mean that fewer workers are needed to produce the same amount of goods. I come from Gary, Indiana, which used to be the home of the world's largest integrated steel mill. On a recent visit to one of the big steel mills in Gary, I was told that while the output was about the same as it was a few decades ago, only one-sixth of the workers are employed. Not surprisingly, Gary looks like a ghost town—like other industrial towns such as Detroit and Akron. Old jobs have been destroyed, but the new jobs have not come. For a while, during the real estate bubble, some of the workers were employed in construction, but that was a distraction, a Band-Aid over the economy's maladies.

Technology Gbbiances [margin note]

This is a tough more complex problem than he gives it credit for [margin note]

It seems strange, in the midst of the Great Recession, when one out of six Americans who would like to get a full-time job is unable to get one, to see stores replacing low-wage cashier clerks with machines. The innovation may be impressive, profits may even be increased, but the broader economic and social consequences cannot be ignored: higher unemployment, lower wages for unskilled labor as the balance of demand and supply tilts more against workers, and greater inequality.

And then there were those innovations of which America was proudest, its financial innovations. Again, that they seemed miraculously to have enhanced the profits of the banks cannot be denied, but neither can it be denied that these financial innovations, which were supposed to help stabilize the economy, did just the opposite. And there is no evidence that they increased overall economic productivity. Indeed the era of financial liberalization and innovation has been a period in which overall growth has been relatively low and a period in which most Americans have faced stagnation.

1980s?! [margin note]

POLITICAL FAILURES

The political system seems to be failing as much as the economic system, and in some ways, the two failures are intertwined. The system failed to prevent the crisis, it failed to remedy the crisis, it failed to check the growing inequality, it failed to protect those at the bottom, and it failed to prevent the corporate abuses. And while it was failing, the growing deficits suggested that these failures were likely to continue into the future.

Earlier, I described how globalization and innovation hadn't brought the promised benefits. But even when markets work as they are supposed to—when workers move from low-productivity protected sectors to higher-productivity export sectors, or when displaced workers succeed in finding alternative employment—economic theory doesn't contend that everyone will be better off. What it says is that the winners *could* compensate the losers, but they seldom do. When the winners are those at the top and the losers are those in the middle and bottom, one might have expected democratic politics to ensure that somehow the benefits would be widely shared. Economic theory only says that the winners *could* compensate the losers, not that they *would*. And in the United States (and many other countries), they haven't. In fact, in some ways, things have been moving the other way, and part of the reason for that has to do with the failure of democratic politics.

Americans, Europeans, and people in other democracies around the world take great pride in their democratic institutions. But the protesters have called into question whether there is a *real* democracy. Real democracy is more than the right to vote once every two or four years. The choices have to be meaningful. The politicians have to listen to the voices of the citizens. However, increasingly, and especially in the United States, it seems that the political system is more akin to "one dollar one vote" than to "one person one vote." Rather the correcting the market's failures, the political system is reinforcing them.

Why? Tax systems in which a billionaire like Warren Buffett pays less taxes (as a percentage of his income) than those who work for him, or in which speculators who helped bring down the global economy are taxed at lower rates than are those who work for their income reinforce the view that politics is unfair, and contribute to the growing inequality. *True*

The failures in politics and economics are related—and they reinforce each other. A political system that amplifies the voice of the wealthy also provides opportunity for laws and regulations—and the administration of laws and regulations—to be designed in ways that not only fail to protect the ordinary citizens against the wealthy but enrich the wealthy at the expense of the rest of society.

ANTI-GLOBALIZATION

In some countries the Occupy Wall Street movement has become closely allied with the anti-globalization movement. They do share some things in common, such as a belief not only that something is wrong but that an alternative world is possible. The Arab Spring, the Occupy Wall Street movement, and the other protests of 2011 have arisen out of globalization and have been successful partly because of globalization—not economic globalization of markets but the globalization of ideas and technology. It was ideas of democracy and a just society, of women's rights and the experiences of so many in the Arab world living in the West that had shown that another world was possible. In his moving essay in this book, Jawad Nabulsi describes how his reading of Malcolm Gladwell convinced him that change was possible—that there was a tipping point and one could nudge society toward that point. Worldwide social networks like Twitter and Facebook allowed the youth to organize themselves, even in the face of police repression. On the wall near the interior ministry in Tunis, painted with graffiti, are thank-you messages to Facebook.

My criticism of globalization lies not with globalization itself, but with the way it has been managed: it is a two-edged sword, and if it is not managed well, the consequences can be disastrous. When managed well—and a few countries have succeeded in managing it well, at least so far—it can bring enormous benefits.

The same is true for the market economy: the power of markets, for good and for evil, is enormous. The increase in productivity and standards of living in the past two hundred years have far exceeded those of the previous two millennia, and markets have played a central role—though so too has government, a fact that free marketers typically fail to acknowledge. But markets have to be tamed and tempered, and that has to be done repeatedly to make sure that they work to the benefit of most citizens. That market control happened in the United States in the progressive era, when competition laws were passed for the first time. It happened during the New Deal, when social security, employment, and minimum wage laws were passed. The message of the Occupy Wall Streeters, and other protesters around the world, was that markets once again needed to be tamed and tempered. Even in parts of the Middle East, where they brought increases in growth, the benefits did not trickle down.

CONCLUDING COMMENTS

More important than the United States' military power is the role that its economic system has played as an aspirational model for the rest of the world. This "soft power," the influence of its ideas and ideals, may be even more important than its economic power. The crisis undermined confidence in that model—and in some ways the protests reflect the resulting dissolution of hope. Something is wrong, but there are no obvious answers, and the old answers are unconvincing.

In many places in the world, confidence in the U.S. economic model has already weakened as the United States, both directly and indirectly through the international institutions that it controlled, has foisted its "market fundamentalist" version of that model on countries around the world. In these countries, the promised benefits didn't materialize. Sometimes there was very little growth. Sometimes there was growth, but it was not sustained. Everywhere where there was growth, the benefits accrued to a few, and where there was pain, it was disproportionately felt by those at the bottom. In Egypt, for instance, growth was not bad between 2004 and 2008—ranging from 4.1 percent to 7.2 percent—but youth unemployment, poverty, and illiteracy remained high. As in the advanced industrial countries, politics and economics reinforced each other. Around the world, political influence, manifested in corrupt privatizations, and anti-competitive practices (often sustained through politics) have been central in creating more unequal societies. And indeed, as I suggested in *Globalization and Its Discontents*, special interests in the United States and other advanced industrial countries played an important role in designing the policies that the international institutions foisted on the developing world, policies that worked well for the elites in both the developed and developing countries.

In more than forty years of travel to developing countries, I have seen these problems at close hand. And throughout 2011, I gladly accepted invitations to Egypt, Spain, and Tunisia, and I met with protesters in Madrid's Retiro Park, at Zuccotti Park in New York, and in Cairo where I spoke with the young men and women who had played a central role at Tahrir Square. As we talked, it was clear to me that they understood how in many ways the system has failed. The protesters have been criticized for not having an agenda, but such criticism misses the point of protest movements. They are an expression of frustration with the electoral process. They are an alarm.

The globalization protests in Seattle in 1999 at what was supposed to be the inauguration of a new round to trade talks called attention to the failures of globalization and the international institutions and agreements that governed it. When the press looked into the allegations, they found that there was more than a grain of truth in these concerns. And as the protests more fully exposed the inequities, popular support gained momentum. The trade negotiations that followed were different because of the protests: at least in principle, they were supposed to be a *development round* to make up for some of these deficiencies. The subsequent reforms of the International Monetary Fund (IMF) too have been significant. These successes echo those of the civil rights protesters of the 1960s who called attention to the ongoing discrimination that was pervasive in American society. No one would argue that the task is over, but President Obama provides testimony to how far things have come.

At one level, these protesters are asking for so little: for a chance to use their skills, for the right to decent work at decent pay, for a fairer economy and society. Their requests are not revolutionary but evolutionary. But at another level, they are asking for a great deal: for a democracy where people, not dollars, matter; and for a market economy that delivers on what it is supposed to do. The two demands are related: unfettered markets do not work well, as we have seen. For markets to work the way markets are supposed to work, there has to be appropriate government regulation. But for that to occur, we have to have a democracy that reflects the general interests, not the special interests. We may have the best government that money can buy, but that won't be good enough.

In some ways, the protesters have already accomplished a great deal: think tanks, government agencies, and the media have confirmed their allegations, of the high and *unjustifiable* level of inequality, the failures of the market system. The expression "we are the 99 percent" has entered into popular consciousness. This book is an attempt to look at this global protest movement through the eyes, and words, of the protesters themselves, letting them speak of their motivations and concerns, of how they organized and the obstacles they face, their hopes and fears. There are similarities but also differences among the accounts in this book. No one can be sure where the Arab Spring or the Occupy Wall Street movements will lead. But of this we can be sure: these young protesters have already altered public discourse and the consciousness of both ordinary citizens and politicians.

EGYPT

OVERVIEW

Jan25. #Tahrir. #KhaledSaid. These social networking hashtags are all shorthand for the most astonishing of all the uprisings of the Arab Spring of 2011: the Egyptian revolution. Egypt, with 81 million people the largest Arab country, had spent thirty long years in the iron grip of President Hosni Mubarak, a former air force officer with a notorious gift for winning elections with 90 percent of the vote. Mubarak had all the makings of a man who was destined to occupy the presidency right until his natural demise, at which point he would probably be able to pass power to a son.

He had it all. A dangerous domestic intelligence network could nip any opposition in the bud. An emergency law in place almost nonstop for forty-four years allowed his regime to abrogate the niceties of the constitution and any civil rights it pleased. And he had the friendship of the United States, which he strengthened by sticking mostly to the superpower's side in regional affairs and by appointing himself the chief prosecutor of the Muslim Brotherhood, an outlawed group that Washington saw as a latent force for extremism and terrorism.

There were signs of stress, surely. Egypt has long been a tumultuous country, famously enduring colonization, multiple revolutions, wars with Israel and Britain, and the assassination of President Anwar Sadat in 1981. In recent years, there were even regular public protests against the government's corruption, rigged elections, and many abuses. But by brutally silencing the most dangerous and the least powerful activists, the regime largely managed to sideline opposition. Activism and civil society were niche pursuits, sometimes even giving Mubarak something to point to as evidence that Egypt was making efforts to open up.

In the late 2000s, though, protests organized by civil society took on a new urgency. Mubarak was growing old; the transfer of power more imminent. The breaking point, probably—though it was not immediately apparent—was the protest movement that emerged following the death of a twenty-eight-year-old Alexandria man, Khaled Said, who was beaten to death by police in June 2010. It was hardly the first time that an Egyptian youth had been killed by police in opaque circumstances for uncertain crimes. But some things had changed by 2010. Most importantly, perhaps, was that Egypt and especially the youth were wired. Said's gruesome postmortem photos made the rounds on social networking sites, on smart phones, and in Internet cafes. This time, the killing was no rumor or the private tragedy of a small community or family. It was documented, and every Egyptian knew about it. Facebook and Twitter activism rallied around Said, often promoted by Egyptians who could now protest without having to reveal their identities. (Some turned out to be quite well connected—the most famous Facebook page, "We are all Khaled Said," was administered by Wael Ghonim, an Egyptian marketing executive for Google.)

It was in the midst of this that Tunisia erupted, and showed the Egyptian protesters—and many who had silently approved but shied away from joining in—that mass nonviolent action could displace even the most entrenched systems of power. With nimble and impressive organizing, activists rallied hundreds of thousands of people to Cairo's aptly named Tahrir ("Liberty") Square on January 25, 2011. Satellite television was there to document it all, and the protests kept growing. The movement was remarkably peaceful, though there were clashes with police and Mubarak supporters who tried to turn things violent—and more than eight hundred people did die. These martyrs, as they were called, only increased the fervor of the protesters. The weeks at Tahrir united a remarkable array of leftists, Islamists, Christians, and the politically unaffiliated, groups that many observers had predicted would never work together. Only eighteen days after the protests began, on February 11, 2011, Hosni Mubarak was forced to step down, and the Egyptian military—a respected institution in the country, at least up until that time—took power.

But the revolution was far from over. Throughout the year, resentment grew toward the military leadership, especially the Supreme Council of the Armed Forces (SCAF), and among the most ardent activists, who had expected much more than trading a dictator for a military state. More large demonstrations erupted in November before the first elections scheduled after Mubarak's fall. Meanwhile, insecurity became a troubling issue—the large minority of Copts felt particularly vulnerable and even targeted for violence. At press time, the elections had been completed relatively free of incidents, with Islamists doing particularly well, but their impact and legitimacy were still somewhat murky.

It seemed that getting rid of Mubarak may have actually been the easy part. But having achieved the unthinkable, and finally tasting freedom, Egyptians justifiably wanted more.

FROM PARTIER TO PROTESTER:
THE BIRTH OF A SOCIAL CONSCIENCE

Jawad Nabulsi

Jawad Nabulsi, twenty-nine, was one of the main figures in the January protests in Tahrir Square that led to the downfall of Egyptian President Hosni Mubarak. Raised in an upper-class family in Cairo, he was educated in Canada and returned home in 2006 to found a network of NGOs (non-governmental organizations) called the Renaissance Council. His work raising funds for poor areas further politicized him, and, using the vast network he had created, Nabulsi went on to help publicize the protests of 2011. Nabulsi, an entrepreneur and partner in different ventures, restaurants, mobile Web sites, and a business incubator, is often referred to as "the pirate" because he wears an eye patch after losing an eye from a police shot on January 28, 2011. He is still involved in the Egyptian youth movement.

Growing up in Egypt, I saw the huge gap that exists between the upper class and the lower class. The middle class in Egypt does not exist; life here is very unfair, and economic injustice seems to be inevitable. My family and I live a privileged life in Egypt, and that made me sympathize with the lower class and understand that the gap between rich and poor needs to be bridged here. We have all noticed the injustice. My great-grandfather originally came from Nablus to Egypt in 1921 and founded a soap factory, which today is still very large. My grandfather was a doctor who studied in Switzerland—something quite rare at the time—and my parents owned an antique business and a restaurant. I lived well; I went to the American school, which was expensive, and we belonged to the exclusive Gezira Club and Heliopolis Club.

People like us had certain opportunities. It was very unfair. When I got my driving license, for example, I didn't do any tests. I just got it. Anything that had to do with the government, people like us had connections so it just got done. Whatever paperwork there was, you'd talk to who you knew in the government or the police and it would be taken care of. Lower-class people had no such opportunities, but I always thought that was how life should be. I was really a bad boy. I got expelled from three schools. I was always having fun and partying. I was a troublemaker. But when I turned seventeen, I wanted a change, so I chose a university in Canada where I could go and make a fresh new start.

I read about Acadia University in Nova Scotia, and since it was the most expensive, I assumed it was the best. I went there in 1999 to study business. There weren't a lot of Arabs or Muslims at Acadia, so people asked me a lot of questions about Middle East politics and the religion of Islam. Before coming to Canada, I hadn't thought much about politics, so I didn't know how to answer all the questions, and that upset me. I began reading and thinking, and found that Canada was a totally different world. In Egypt we thought Palestinians had the right to land, but in Canada people thought the opposite, that it was the Palestinians who were the aggressors. I started reading and learning about the Middle East. I read Norman Finkelstein, Israel Shahak, Mohamed Hassanein Heikal, and Ahmed Dajani. I had never met a Jew before, and I thought they were all murderers, but I learned there was a difference between Zionists and Jews. I started an Arabic students association, and there were Jews who joined because they were against the Israeli occupation in Palestine. I began lecturing every Friday, and more and more people came. Talking about these topics helped me learn about them.

Then September 11th happened, and I began talking to so many people on campus. I'd drop into classes I wasn't enrolled in, and when 9/11 came up, I would jump into the discussion. I'd explain that all Muslims are not terrorists and neither are the Palestinians. I was exposed to so many ideas, especially when I began volunteering for Canadian election campaigns. In 2003, I worked on Peter McKay's campaign for leadership of the Progressive Conservative Party. (He now serves as Canada's Minister of National Defence.) I met Prime Minister Steven Harper. I helped the New Democratic Party. I had no agenda. I just wanted to learn and talk to people about the Arab situation.

I kept looking at Egypt and thinking, "Why do we have a president who has been there for thirty years, and I can see there is no chance for me to be in power? In all of the Arab world, what is the chance of this happening? I can see almost none." In Egypt, you had to abide by the ideologies of those in power and accept a certain level of corruption. In Canada it was different. Being an Arab, I was occasionally harassed and beaten up, but the police and so many people were sympathetic to me even though they were white and Christian. The people who beat me up were fined and put on academic probation. It was an eye opener. I realized I couldn't generalize about people. I learned not to judge anyone until I had seen them up close. You can't always trust what you read in the newspaper. You have to get information yourself.

Talking about democracy is one thing. Seeing it in action is something else. People said to me, "The Middle East has poverty and corruption," and I thought, "Look at all the prophets from our part of the world. We can't be that bad. Jesus, Moses, and Muhammed came from our part of the world so we can't be that bad." I formed a foundation called Lifemakers Canada, and we had a campaign around the world to send used clothes to Darfur and Palestine. I organized groups all over Canada, and we filled 10 forty-foot containers of clothing—cleaned, folded, and packed. But I realized at the end of the day that if I wanted to reach people, it would not be in Canada but in my own country. Life is already pleasant in Canada. They did not need my help. The challenge was to come back, use what I had learned, and bring it to Egypt.

In 2006, I came back to Egypt and met with non-governmental organizations (NGOs) working in different fields. I formed a council of NGOs called the Renaissance Council, and we held weekly coordination meetings. I began working in Upper Egypt and saw that the quality of services there was totally different. It just was not fair. Salaries were about E£70 to E£80 a month, or $15 to $20, and there was no water or electricity in the houses. It was like these villages were in the Stone Age. It wasn't right. We raised money and used it to pay the water and electricity company to connect these villagers to water and electricity, but then the government began privatizing, and the cost of connecting homes doubled. I was outraged. The people were so poor. I can't describe how callous this price increase was. I felt it was extremely unjust. But we started getting a better idea of what the needs were and what had to be done. I also started an environmental awareness group called Keep Egypt Clean, which now has more than a hundred thousand members. We all kept in touch on Facebook, and I developed a huge network.

I had gone to villages and slums, had seen the depth of problems in these places, and assumed they could not be fixed. I'd tell myself, "They are too humongous. It's like throwing something in the sea." Then I read *The Tipping Point* by Malcolm Gladwell and understood you don't need to change the whole population. You just need a few people. I realized I needed to bring together a circle of key players who could have an influence. I also read *Good to Great: Why Some Companies Make the Leap and Others Don't* by Jim Collins. It reinforced the idea that it's not about the people in the company; it's about the *right* people in the company. I didn't need to change everything, I just needed to focus on the leaders in the community and work with them.

Around this time, so many things happened. In 2008, my brother, who was religious but not political, was picked up by the police and tortured. It was just dumb luck that I wasn't home at 3 A.M. when the police broke down the door, or I would have been arrested too. They detained him under the emergency laws, so they could keep him for forty days without a trial before he had to be released.

All across Egypt, you could feel that people were ready for a change. Everyone knew someone who had been arrested or had had to pay a bribe—even relatives of the police. I'd take a taxi or a bus, and everyone was talking about how fed up they were, how things had to change. I remember meeting a soldier who had been standing for twelve hours on the street in case the president's car passed by. He was so angry. How could Mubarak think people would defend him? This *was* the tipping point. Everyone felt the same way about the police and the government, and when they got on Facebook, they found other people to listen to them. They got information, and they could make their own decisions. The balance tipped. Going down to protest became acceptable. Before then, people like members of my family would have said, "No way, how could you protest? It is not something people like us do." Then it became normal to protest. It became something we *could* do.

Right after Tunisia, the call for protests in Egypt had started. We didn't know we could collapse the regime, but we knew something good would happen. I was sitting with someone close to the regime, and I told him, "This time it's different. You will see."

When we started organizing for the January 25 "Day of Anger," we knew something big would happen, something unprecedented, but we never thought the president would go to jail. We didn't think. We just went down to the streets and called others to join us. People just kept coming, and the crowd got bigger and bigger

until we saw there was no turning back. Going to Tahrir Square
was a risk, and there was no way we could come back.

I was not an organizer. I was a lobbyist. There were so many
people in different groups and with different backgrounds, and
they called online for us to protest. Because I already knew a lot of
people, I just spread the word to different leftist organizations and
groups against the police brutality. I told people we would meet
at the Mustapha Mahmoud Mohandessein 29th mosque. We saw
soldiers who didn't know why we were there, and we wanted to get
their support, so I hugged them and told them, "We are doing this
for you. We need justice." It was so emotional. We were hugging
and crying.

Walking around Tahrir Square, we saw most people were not like
us. They were not educated or informed, and a lot of them tried to
disrupt things. Some even tried to steal. But we had enough of a
tipping point to prevent any fighting or harming anyone, and that
made our protest peaceful. If we saw anyone trying to break anything, we would tell them to stop. We saw abandoned police cars,
and there were policeman nearby. People wanted to kill them. To
prevent this from happening, I went up to the officers and encouraged them to take off their uniforms and run away.

There were women and young children in the square. Without
women, this protest would not have been possible. I saw a lady
with tear gas in her eyes, and she would not stop marching. I saw
women getting shot with rubber bullets, and they would continue.
The women were amazing. If there is to be a renaissance in this
part of the world, it will be from women, not men. The women
will lead.

On January 28, between 11 P.M. and midnight, I got shot several
times, and a bullet went into my eye. It took me twelve hours to get
treatment; I could barely walk, and I was passing out. My friends
held onto me and protected me. The police and the army were still
in the square, and it was so dangerous to be there, especially in my
condition.

I was moved from hospital to hospital on the back of someone's motor bike. Moving around the city, I met different protesters who didn't have money, and I took their names and numbers. A few days later, when I was released from the hospital, I set up a call center to take information about people who were wounded or missing. I announced the number on my Web site so people could call and volunteer to help. I also reached out to TV channels, asking them to broadcast the number so people could call in. Still weak from my injuries, I printed thousands of leaflets with the URL of the Web site and passed them around at Tahrir Square.

There was so much going on during that time. President Mubarak made a mistake. He gave an emotional speech against the revolution, saying he was old and would give up power at the end of the year. His supporters and the police hired thugs, and they went to Tahrir Square and tried to kick the people out. I could see members of the secret police everywhere. But their violence made people sympathetic to us. Mubarak's supporters just didn't get it. It's the same thing going on again right now. The violence won people over to our side. The silent majority started to sympathize with the protesters in Tahrir Square, and this is when you win. You just have to stand long enough so that the silent majority is on your side. But if you don't win the silent majority, there won't be a tipping point. You won't effect change. The people sympathized with us, and the army knew there was no way they could be violent against us, so Mubarak stepped down. Then there was a celebration, and the anger and frustration in the streets transformed into jubilation.

When you say something for so long and it actually happens, it's weird. It gives you so much confidence. The Egyptian people are in a totally different place now because of this confidence. We feel that if we can do something as momentous as eliminating the regime, we can eliminate poverty and illiteracy. There is a huge gap between us and the older generation because we saw the revolution happen. The Internet exposed us to so many ideas so we could make our own analysis and our own decisions.

Things are going to work out. It's a process. The regime is still there, but the time has come for change. No one is untouchable. Everyone can make mistakes, and everyone has to be accountable. Anyone who thinks he is in his position because of his brain or his power or his money is in for a rude awakening. This arrogance will be broken down. It's about justice.

THE REVOLUTIONARY ROAD
STARTS IN TUNISIA

Lina Attalah

Lina Attalah is editor of Egypt Independent, *a news Web site published by Al-Masry Al-Youm.*

Like many of us, I wasn't revolutionary enough to expect the revolution. Early on in the week of January 25, 2011, my brain was preoccupied with Tunisia, where a revolt had just toppled Zine El Abidine Ben Ali's twenty-three-year rule. On my long drive through Cairo's foggy landscape to our newsroom every morning, I kept hearing a voice inside me nudging, "Can you imagine a Tunisia without Ben Ali?" All I could think about was showing up in Tunis just to bear witness.

On one level, my longing to land in revolutionary Tunisia could be reduced to sheer political tourism, but there was a deeper reason for the impulse. Scenes of ordinary Tunisians' outbursts on the country's streets and squares summoned a whole new array of possibilities. The energy and spontaneity of the movement brought home the fact that revolution is not just some abstract notion incarcerated in history books; it's not something that only happens elsewhere, far away from home. It is a reality that is unfolding here and now, and its new meaning can be appropriated by us all. Its frontiers lie at our very doorstep.

But I didn't know it yet. I was so un-revolutionary in my thinking that my newspaper articles and Twitter timeline were abundant with theories on why Egypt was not Tunisia, on why Egypt would not revolt: "we're too many," "we're uneducated," and "we have just enough of a false margin of freedom that tames us and keeps us from agitating for change." I'd just had a thorough conversation with my friend about how the Mubarak regime had butchered the pro-democracy movement after 2005. Back then, a relative political opening unfolded at home, and protesters grew vocal against the government, but it wasn't long before they were detained. Mubarak deployed some cosmetic reforms, putting a subtle closure to the unborn revolution.

Little could I see of the contradiction laid out between these two lines of thought. As unexpected and surprising as Tunisia's revolution was, we put so much effort into not expecting our own revolution in Egypt. And, as we later learned, we must imagine the impossible for it to become possible.

BEYOND OUR DOORSTEP: THE WIND REACHES EGYPT

Fixated on my (failed) plan to be in Tunisia, I never properly organized the coverage of the January 25 protests, which were intended to counter the regime's celebration of Police Day. This security apparatus became the face of the police state we'd lived under for decades. Its ultimate demise became the point of departure for the demand to topple the regime.

In our relatively small newsroom, we were caught off guard. As the day progressed, some of us experimented with taking to the streets and being among the crowds, while others went home thinking it was just one more protest that would soon be curbed by the police. I ended up on the street, just a block away from our newspaper's offices. A sea of people stormed the street from different sides to the rhythmic chant of *"al-shaab yurid isqat al-nizam"* (the people want the fall of the regime). The chant bore through the grand and heavy silence that has for so long brought my city down. I now know I was watching a revolution unfold.

Early in the battle with the police, we were chased with water cannons and tear gas. As I ran, I found myself pulled from the back by my hair and dragged on the ground. Four policemen surrounded me, beating every part of my body with batons, all the while hurling a storm of verbal abuse. A first punch into my face broke my glasses to pieces, and along with them the sight of chaos faded away as I slowly numbed to the physical pain, and the sound pollution of insults merged into the general din. An embattled ancien régime was breaking down before my eyes, and that was its final *adieux*.

Later that day, as I lay in my hospital bed, I learned that the revolutionaries were advancing toward Tahrir Square. The two days that followed were a series of street battles in Cairo, while the people of Suez, east of Cairo, were already defeating the police. As I was watching the regime's imminent demise, I thought of the physical assault I was subjected to as bearing the traces of our ongoing battle with the police state. This was everyone's fight.

In my nine-year career as a journalist in Egypt, I was never preoccupied with the frontiers that divide journalism from activism. Seeking the truth in a police state was already a de facto form of activism. Journalism was our civic engagement; voyeurism was a crime. At the *Egypt Independent*, I work with a team of young journalists whose bravery in covering the eighteen days to come, and the days that followed, has been both motivating and humbling. Together, we vowed through our coverage to be engaged and immersed while challenging the prevalent narratives. So the fight was also ours to win or lose.

THE WRATH RESTS IN TAHRIR

By the "Friday of Wrath," January 28, Egyptians had assigned themselves a revolution. We woke to a Cairo that was like a ghost town, cut off from the rest of the world after the regime jammed all means of communications, including mobile telephones and the Internet. We were left with nothing but landlines and plenty of determination to both revolt and cover the revolt. We called our friends overseas, gave them our Web site passwords, and tasked them with posting our phone feeds. We'd heard of a hotel in downtown where an Internet service provider was still working, so we stormed it and congregated in one of its rooms, turning it into a makeshift newsroom. Little did we know another eighteen days would elapse before we could regroup in full force in our actual newsroom at the *Egypt Independent* headquarters. By prayer time, we had dispersed into the different mosques and squares of the city.

Within seconds after the crowds finished their Friday prayers, they were showered with tear gas and water cannons. Within hours some of our team members were forced out of the protest by the atrocities of the police, who were deploying the brutal tactics of sheer madness to survive. One of my colleagues was arrested and kept for hours in a police truck that was eventually set on fire by protesters who did not realize there were detainees inside. He later told me he was certain he was going to die in that blaze and started mentally listing the names of his loved ones, apologizing to each of them in his mind for not bidding them a proper farewell. Another member of our team was taken to prison, alongside hundreds of protesters and journalists, but walked out when the gates broke open. Prisoners were forced out in the regime's desperate attempt to unleash a chaos that would undermine the revolution.

Back in our makeshift newsroom at the hotel, we frantically posted news and photos. A hodgepodge of contradictory sentiments fueled us, from extreme fear to renewed hope. We watched the historical events unfold from our balcony, which offered us a close-up view of what became a visual symbol and a microcosm of the revolution: the Battle of Qasr al-Nil Bridge. Otherwise known as "lover's bridge" in everyday Cairo, this was the site of a daylong confrontation between hundreds of thousands of protesters and the police force. On this long bridge that spans the Nile, masses emerged from Cairo's different quarters and kept advancing despite the police's storm of live bullets. The revolutionaries eventually won and moved on to the square, Tahrir, where the wrath was contained and took the form of occupation.

REVOLUTION AS EVERYDAY

On January 29, I took a drive through the rubble that was what had become of an angry Cairo. My city still reeked from the smell of burnt-out buildings and vehicles. Things seemed to have gone back to the basics, in a quest for a new beginning. Amidst the wreckage, Cairo's landscape looked somewhat serene.

For days to follow, we lived through an enacted dream in Tahrir Square—a model city that bounced between the festive and the political every day. In the morning, we "covered" Tahrir; in the evening, we tried to live it. Covering and living Tahrir meant negotiating our way through an array of new political notions: regime fall, state survival, military intervention, the revolutionaries' demands, and most importantly, the reinvigoration of the political in the Egyptian everyday. While we passionately wrote and photographed the details of life in the square, from makeshift hospitals to media tents to exhibits of the martyrs' photos, we also delved into how the politicians of a demised regime decoded this sudden outbreak of anger against them.

One day, I woke up early in the square and sat calmly by our tent to smoke a morning cigarette and contemplate our model city. As some jogged around the square to the chants of *"al-shaab yurid isqat al-nizam,"* and others roamed around offering campers tea and biscuits, I found two veiled girls sitting close to me. They looked new to the square and seemed disoriented but curious nevertheless. When I returned their smiles, they came and asked me if I really thought the regime would fall because of this sit-in. I smiled again and asked them what brought them to the square. They said that they went to an art school and their professor, Ahmad Basiony, was killed in the early days of the uprising by police. They came to see what he died for. The sound of the name *Basiony*, whose artwork I knew and admired, pierced my ears.

Covering and living Tahrir also brought a plethora of personal discoveries. Suddenly we were free to explore the body politic outside the previous context of high regulation. We challenged our boundaries of risk, unveiling the revolution within ourselves. Our journalism throughout the days that followed January 28 became what I now consider a historic record of the square's emotional history. We were chronicling the ebbs and flows of hope, desperation, persistence, boredom, fear, and jubilation. In short, we were documenting the human face of revolution.

On February 12, just hours after Mubarak left power, we wrestled between the urge to take time off to join in the celebration and staying behind our desks to write an editorial. We ended up writing an editorial titled, "The Revolution Begins Now." We wrote to the world and to ourselves that the seeming end of the revolt with Mubarak's ouster was fake, and that the ensuing battle would be a simultaneous undoing and doing.

After February, our team traveled everywhere from Bahrain to Syria to Libya to cover the unfolding revolution elsewhere, an act of commitment that stamped our memory with the fact that revolutions are both contagious and borderless. We would always come back with stories and hope.

Today, back in Egypt, our revolution stands at a crossroads. Marred by the challenges of the counterrevolution and the attempts of reactionary and conservative forces to steal it, we live through the constantly changing tides of revolt. As I write these words, my ears are still filled with the sounds of shutters banging on downtown Cairo's storefronts. For the last week, street battles between the revolutionaries and the police have claimed more than forty lives under the rule of a military junta that is struggling to believe that the revolution is over.

A few weeks earlier, their armored vehicles ran over protesters in a march organized by Copts and activists, killing at least twenty-eight. Our martyrs are falling by the dozens, but they are more than numbers. Through our newspaper, we recall their names and faces so well, for they drive our revolution forward. Today the chant *"al-shaab yurid isqat al-nizam"* has come back to the square, resonating beyond its border. Our revolution is against the faces of oppression, backwardness, and conservatism, be it in the person of Mubarak or in a military uniform or under the cover of a pious beard.

"We shall be victorious," are the resonating words of my friend Alaa Abd El Fattah, a renowned activist who was in a military prison. His imprisonment sums up the difficulties of the revolutionary process. His expression, however, is a reminder that hope is a revolutionary obligation.

TUNISIA

OVERVIEW

In a region where the repressed discontent of the masses has often been described as combustible, it is hard to think of a more apt beginning than Tunisia's to the revolutions that spread like wildfire through Arab countries in the winter and spring of 2011. On December 17, 2010, Mohammed Bouazizi, a poor twenty-six-year-old fruit seller from the small city of Sidi Bouzid, doused himself in gasoline and lit himself aflame. Humiliated by police who had confiscated his fruits and harassed him for years—culminating, it was said, in a public slap from a policewoman—Bouazizi protested unaccountable power by sacrificing the only thing he had left: his own life and body.

His action immediately resonated in Tunisia and beyond, at least partly because Bouazizi personified the problems of his generation. He was young—27 percent of Tunisians are fifteen to twenty-nine, mirroring a youth bulge throughout North Africa and the Middle East. He was underemployed in a country where the official unemployment rate was 14 percent, and the reality—especially for youth—was much worse. He lacked meaningful opportunities—he dreamed of a university education but could never finish high school, instead struggling to support his family of eight with the pittance he made from his street vending.

Worst of all, he had no way, official or otherwise, to even try to effect change.

Within days of Bouazizi setting himself on fire, Tunisians began filling the streets of their cities with largely peaceful protests. Simply assembling in such great numbers was an audacious act of defiance in a country whose president-for-life, Zine El Abidine Ben Ali—like so many regional despots—had systematically crushed dissent through decades of spying on his own citizens. But Tunisians were doing more than assembling—they were calling for revolution: the departure of the president and his cronies, the dismantling of the state security service that did the president's bidding, and a better constitution. Aided by the organizing powers of Facebook and the Internet, by January 14—less than a month after the incident at Sidi Bouzid—they had accomplished the first objective. A little more than a month later, they were well on their way to accomplishing the other two. On February 27, Ben Ali's long-time prime minister, Mohamed Ghannouchi, had also resigned, and elections were called for a Constituent Assembly that would work on the constitution.

This display of mass nonviolent action to effect rapid change would have been stunning anywhere, but it was especially remarkable in a region that had grown notorious for its seeming inability to change peacefully, if at all. But if there was anyone surprised about the fact that Tunisia was ripe for revolt, and enacted one first, it wasn't most Tunisians. Ben Ali had cultivated an image as a relatively forward-thinking leader in the West, one of those more or less benevolent semi-dictators that Washington and Paris seemed to think might be just good enough for the Arabs. On the face of things, Ben Ali kept up respectable economic growth rates for Tunisia and allowed opposition parties to exist. If some Islamists disappeared from time to time, no one was going to make much of a fuss.

Tunisians knew better. What gains were being made were going to the well-connected. The opposition had its wings clipped, and

it was hardly just the Islamists who suffered repression. People—
especially the youth—were angry. The Internet gave them new
opportunities to communicate with each other and discover how
widespread dissatisfaction really was, and what could be done
about it.

So finally, more or less spontaneously and en masse, they decided to risk their lives to make a change. It worked, and the
world took note. Ben Ali fled to Saudi Arabia with his wife, Leila
Ben Ali. In absentia, they have both been sentenced to thirty-five
years in prison for their misrule and corruption. His party, the
Constitutional Democratic Rally (RCD), was disbanded in May,
and bans on other parties were dropped. Elections were held in
October, and the moderate Islamist party Ennahada took control
of the new Constituent Assembly.

Tunisia has not found solutions to all its economic woes, nor an
answer to every question about its future. But of all the countries
of the Arab Spring, this first to revolt seems now to have been the
most successful at turning the corner and entering a new era of
peaceful democracy.

OUT FROM BEHIND THE SUN

Mouheb Ben Garoui

Mouheb Ben Garoui, twenty-four, is a co-founder and the president of the I-Watch organization, a Tunis-based advocate for governmental and political transparency and accountability that serves as an anti-corruption government watchdog. He received his degree in international relations and English from the Higher Institute of Human Sciences in Tunis in 2011. A participant in the World Affairs Middle East and North Africa (MENA) Democracy Fellows Program, he was a fellow at the office of U.S. Representative Keith Ellison (D-MN) through October 2011, and conducted research on political finance in Tunisia with MENA and the Applied Research Center at the International Foundation of Electoral Systems (IFES) through November 2011.

Zine El Abidine Ben Ali's rule couldn't have started more appropriately: it began, on November 7, 1987, with a lie. The then–prime minister took power in a peaceful *coup d'état*, claiming President Habib Bourguiba was too sick to lead. In reality, it was just the first of many crass power grabs that served our leader and not Tunisians.

Many Tunisians believed that and countless other lies that followed. As a result, for twenty-three years we suffered corruption, terror, and injustice from our government.

By the time people realized that they had been fooled, it was too late to do anything. Ben Ali had built a dense network of domestic spies—and a system of extrajudicial punishments—that kept the country in line with fear. Just as the knowledge that we lived under an unjust regime had seeped into each Tunisian's subconscious, so did the understanding that we must never utter a peep. Those who did paid with their lives or their freedom. There are no exact figures about the killings that took place before the revolution, but all the international watchdog organizations have confirmed that more than thirty thousand Islamists were sent to jail in the 1990s, and the leaders were exiled. Oppressing prisoners, raping men and women, and firing workers were some of the famous tools of Ben Ali's police. Resistance meant suppression with violence, as happened in a 2008 uprising in Redeyef. The police killed dozens there, though there was no media coverage or international response.

How did a nation paralyzed by fear for a quarter century start the revolution that would send the winds of change across the entire Arab world? Even to me, trying to look back a year later—as we Tunisians continue barreling forward into the unknown—the answer is something of a mystery. What is clear is that there was a breaking point when private dissatisfaction transformed into public resistance. And once released, the bird of our aspiration soared high and could not again be caged. I can only look at my own story and search for the place where I moved from silence to words and action. That break came for Tunisians as individuals and as a nation.

In the decades before the revolution, which seem distant now, most of us never dared to imagine another order. There were some opposition parties, political and human rights activists calling for a better Tunisia, but they were not strong enough to face Ben Ali's huge political machine. We were instinctively self-censoring from a young age. When people of my generation were children, our parents occasionally had to remind us that Big Brother was watching. At the dinner table, in the privacy of our homes, we quickly learned the kneejerk response to a comment or innocent question about the president or his party, the Constitutional Democratic Rally (RCD). "Shh! The walls are listening!" My parents taught me not to talk politics, not to criticize, and not to think. They did it because they loved me: they were afraid that the feared political police would send me *behind the sun*, the term used for those critics of Ben Ali who were disappeared. The mindset, however, was self-defeating. Tunisia itself gradually became a big jail.

The fear haunted me. But as I grew into a thinking person, against the odds perhaps, I knew that my country deserved better. I started rebelling in the tiniest ways.

In 2006, at the age of nineteen, I moved from my hometown of Kairouan in the central part of the country to Tunis, the capital, to attend university studying the English language and literature. There, I was assigned to live in a public dorm. When they gave me my room key, I discovered that I was going to live on the sixth floor in a dorm without a working elevator, in a tiny room crammed with three people. There were five hundred in the building. Rats scurried in the rooms; restrooms and four showers were dirty and shared by all five hundred students, and there were periodic all-day power cuts.

My father called me later and asked how things were going. When I told him the story of my dorm, he was very angry. His solution: I should go and register in the RCD. Then I could join the nearly one million other Tunisians—about 10 percent of the population—who were card carriers. Most, it was assumed, joined not because they shared the party's political vision—whatever that was supposed to be—but to enjoy special privileges and, especially, to get jobs. My father, a government employee and thus RCD member himself,[12] reckoned that the first of the privileges that I would enjoy would be a nice room on a lower floor. He was right. This was where all the RCD students lived in relative style, two to a room and without any electricity cuts, which affected only floors three and above.

I refused. My father argued with me, but I held my ground. My parents' expectations for me in school and in my professional life were very high. Like many Tunisian parents, they feared that I might neglect my studies at the expense of the political notions that they could sense were bubbling up within me.

My father shouted at me, but eventually he relented. At the time, it felt like an isolated and impulsive moment of taking a stand for a principle. As it turned out, it was an incident that marked a turning point in my life. I was torn between the words of my father and reality on one side, and my principles on the other. Choosing the latter, I took a path that would lead to revolution, though I hardly knew it then.

On the sixth floor, I spent the best moments in my life. I lived with ordinary students who, like me—and unlike the RCD students on the first two floors—opposed Ben Ali in secret. Sometimes we would talk to each other about our political ideas, but we had to be careful because the RCD had student spies in universities and dorms who wrote reports about those who opposed the regime. But this situation created a sense of unity among underprivileged students.

That year, I started reading *Al Mawkef* (*The Position*), a weekly newspaper owned by the most famous opposition party at that time, *Parti Démocratique Progressiste*, or PDP. (Probably for the sake of keeping up appearances, Ben Ali had allowed the party to exist, but its activities were severely curtailed, and getting involved was still risky.) I started discovering what was really going on behind the scenes, and it was a total break with the mainstream Tunisian media, which described the country as a haven of democracy and freedom of speech, free from killings and kangaroo courts. That message might have convinced some tourists and foreigners, but almost every Tunisian knew it was false. Even so, we didn't know, in specific terms, how corrupt our government was. I read the newspaper in secret—even though it was legally published, we all knew that Ben Ali allowed it mostly in order see who was buying it and reading it. If informants noticed you bought it on a regular basis, they would start following you. So I read it in my room, and at the back of the classroom with my friend Achref.[13] We were discovering the atrocities that Ben Ali and his forces were committing, and we were debating some taboo political issues. The fear gradually started to dissipate.

Later, I took my criticizing activities to the Web, where I used a proxy—software that broke the censorship on Web sites that criticized Ben Ali. I enjoyed venting. But at a certain point I wondered, "Is this how I am going to fight against Ben Ali? Is this how I am going to change my country?" The answer, of course, was "No." Internet activism may have started the ferment, but it could not by itself bring real change. I debated with myself whether to sacrifice my studies and my future and fight against Ben Ali now or finish my studies and get a job and then start my opposition in public.

Then came December 17, 2010. A now-famous twenty-six-year-old in Sidi Bouzid (a small city in the south of Tunisia) named Mohammed Bouazizi immolated himself after being slapped in the face by a policewoman. People said that he was humiliated by the authorities after they refused to give him permission to sell fruits and vegetables in the market.

From that moment, the questions and doubts I had about revolt—and that many young Tunisians shared—were erased forever. The revolution had begun, sweeping from the south to north of the country like a steady, unstoppable wave.

When Bouazizi set himself aflame, I was in Tunis. I knew about the events in Sidi Bouzid from Facebook—Tunisian media was very silent, and then misleading, reporting that the police were trying to put down riots in the south started by some "terrorists and gangs." I didn't believe it, and on Facebook I watched videos of protesters chanting famous opposition songs that I used to hear some students sing in my university. The uprising spread to Gasserine, Gafsa, Sfax, and Gabes in the southern part of the country. When it reached Kairouan, I decided to go home. I wanted to be with my friends, and if something was going to happen to me, I would rather die in my hometown. I returned on January 11. *No way to go back*, I thought. *It's now or never.* I started posting protesters' videos and photos of martyrs and injured protesters on my Facebook page.

My concerns about my personal future evaporated. All that mattered were the innocent people being killed and accused of being gang members and terrorists. By the time I returned to Kairouan, protests had just begun to reach Tunis. I knew because I saw clashes between police and demonstrators downtown on my way to the bus station. Kairouan was in a state of revolt. My parents were still cautious; my mother was begging me not to go outside. Snipers were everywhere, and the police were using force to disperse the protesters in every street. Everything was closed—cafés, restaurants, and shops. Down every lane, one could find only the military and the police. When a friend called me and told me that the labor union (General Union of Tunisian Workers, or UGTT) was organizing a big protest, I joined them. I had to ignore my mother's calls to my mobile phone as we took to the streets—and indeed, this was a moment when all young Tunisians had to turn their backs on the warnings of parents who loved them. My friends and I posted pictures and videos to Facebook, showing that more than twenty thousand protesters had flooded the streets of my city of some three hundred thousand.

I participated in every protest in Kairouan from that day until Ben Ali fled the country on January 14—the biggest milestone in the revolution. After that, my parents knew that I would not go back. They stopped asking me to stay home and just asked me to take care when I left in the mornings. They still didn't support my objectives, though. It was all too dangerous.

I went back to Tunis. The air was electric. Suddenly throngs of once silent or surreptitiously critical people were filling the streets, apparently having gone through a transformation similar to mine. Almost all the protesters were young. We demanded that Ben Ali's prime minister, Mohamed Ghannouchi, step down. When he refused, protesters staged a sit-in in front of his office in late January to ask him to resign, but the sit-in was broken up by police forces. Another sit-in was organized later in February, calling for Constituent Assembly elections and the resignation of Ghannouchi. After two weeks, on February 27, we were successful, and Ghannouchi resigned after eleven years in power. The same night, interim President Foued Mbazaa called for Constituent Assembly elections. Then we decided to end the sit-in.

Through it all, it was an organic movement that brought a diverse group of Tunisians together. The UGTT may have played a role in organizing—the rumors were that they provided protesters with banners, food, and tents—but the union never said so in public, and in reality, political parties never influenced the sit-in, and their banners were nowhere to be seen. Rather, it was ordinary people who came by the thousands from Sidi Bouzid, Gafsa, Gasserine, and Kairouan to participate in this protest.

We had never felt such energy. The walls of our great jail had been broken down. Many of us have been ceaselessly active since. In my case, my friend Achref called me in late February, when the revolution was hardly over, and told me of his idea of creating a watchdog organization to fight against corruption in Tunisia. Nine months later, I-Watch has chapters in seven cities. We have observed the elections that took place on October 23, with more than five hundred observers deployed in different polling stations around the country, and now we are focusing on accountability and transitional justice. All the leaders of this organization are between twenty and twenty-five years old. Many other young Tunisians have also directed their fervor to projects rebuilding our country. No one is taking our new liberties for granted, and some still need convincing this is the right path. My parents, for instance, are still wary of my efforts to end corruption. They think it remains too risky a pursuit. I have not had political discussions with them, and my father especially remains very pragmatic.

Mostly, though, that bottled-up desire for freedom and justice has proved larger and more powerful than anyone predicted. And while our insurrection was not armed, our energy is a fierce one. Westerners have called our uprising the "Jasmine Revolution," but this term doesn't describe the forceful break from the past we have made. Tunisians call it the "Dignity Revolution." We believe that dignity was the unique demand of those who protested all around the country and occupied the streets, and in many cases gave their lives—some three hundred were killed. The threat of being thrown "behind the sun" had taken much from us, but our dignity could not be crushed. As we lost more and more over the years, I think dignity became the main thing we cared about. Economics didn't matter (even if Ben Ali had turned our economy into a sham). What we wanted was political. Our motto in the streets was "Bread and water and no to Ben Ali." That meant we didn't care about money; we just needed him to leave.

Now, Tunisians have a responsibility not only to their country but also to the whole region. The waves of freedom started from Tunisia and washed over the rest of the Arab world. We are leading the revolutions, and we should lead by example. Our lesson to the world is this: we accomplished revolution by ourselves—we toppled Ben Ali and the dictatorship—and now we can build democracy by ourselves, too. For my part, I hope that my efforts with I-Watch, the first Tunisian youth watchdog organization, will also evolve into the first youth think tank organization in the history of the country.

I hope we can change our country for the benefit of the coming generations. The Tunisian Constitutional Assembly has started working on the constitution that will define the main principles for the future of Tunisia. It is now all of our jobs to participate in writing the next chapter of our country and to make sure we never become tools in the hands of a dictator, as we were for so long with Ben Ali. I don't want my son or daughter blaming me for missing the opportunity to change Tunisia. I hope we can decrease unemployment rates, especially among young graduate students. We want safety, less corruption, less opportunism, and more optimism. That may take five or ten years. But no matter what it takes, we have to persevere. We fought for dignity and freedom, and we'll never forgive, nor forget the old regime's attempt to rob us of those.

INTERNET ACTIVISM, TUNISIAN STYLE

Haythem El Mekki

Haythem El Mekki, twenty-nine, is a Tunisian journalist and blogger who appeared on the scene after the Tunisian revolution as one of the new media figures. Known for his frank observations and activism on the Web, he currently works for Tunisian National TV and for Radio Mosaïque FM, the first private radio station in the country.

The Tunisian Revolution was all about *actocracy*, as in "let the one who holds the brush decide the color of the wall she paints." Nothing was planned; no movement was organized. As most people now know, everything began on December 17, 2010, in Sidi Bouzid in the center of the country, where a young man, Tarak (Mohammed) Bouazizi, set himself on fire in protest against the municipal police, who had prevented him from carrying on his un-authorized itinerant grocery business and confiscated his wares. But few realize that he was not the first one to do so. On March 3, 2010, Abdesselem Trimech, another street vendor from Monastir, burned himself in front of the municipality for the same reason. It was all about unemployment, poverty, and segregation between the coast and the interior regions of the country—the same problems that sparked the Redeyef unrest in the mining area of Gafsa in 2008.

Demonstrations had begun in Sidi Bouzid almost to the moment of Bouazizi's self-immolation. Even though he was not especially popular in the community, his act symbolized the sense of outrage and desperation that had been felt for some time. People were compelled to stand up for their rights once and for all. As soon as the authorities heard about the movement, the police came in and the repression was so violent that once-peaceful demonstrations turned into all-out riots.

At that time, I was working as assistant to the editor-in-chief of an online magazine, Tunivisions.net. Ben Ali's regime had total control of media, so almost no one wrote about Bouazizi. But, according to our boss, we had a duty to do so. We had to take advantage of our only weapon, the biggest open and free media in the world: the Internet.

Some Internet citizens, bloggers, and cyberactivists immediately started reporting. Pages were created on Facebook especially for coverage, like "Smile a lot, you're not from Sidi Bouzid" and "People of Tunisia are burning themselves, Mr. President." On Twitter, the hashtag #SidiBouzid was created to follow up the movement. Though Facebook is used by everyone, Twitter is kind of an elitist network in Tunisia, and there were not more than two thousand members at the time, but many on Twitter were well-known activists, journalists, and bloggers, which made them very efficient in spreading the news worldwide. I was following the whole movement closely and trying my best to participate while focusing on raising awareness, and showing everyone what our immediate responses to the situation should be.

On Facebook, a handful of people started sharing the videos and information coming out of Sidi Bouzid. Soon after, the police surrounded the town and cut off access to the Internet. Coverage became next to impossible, but the revolutionaries quickly found another way to send the data out of town, via USB drives. People would shoot the videos with their cell phones, and instead of uploading them on the Internet, they put them on thumb drives and smuggled them out of town with the help of travelers. Some drivers of public transport vehicles such as the *louage*, which is a kind of between-towns taxi that goes back and forth many times a day from Sidi Bouzid to Tunis, took a huge personal risk and performed a service that was essential in bringing the struggle to the light.

Azyz Amami, a young activist and blogger originally from Sidi Bouzid, was one of the most important sources of information through the first days of the uprising. His family and friends, who were among the first to suffer from repression, were providing him with updates and videos that he published on TwitVid. Internet surfers downloaded the data from there and kept uploading it on Facebook. Unfortunately, the most important part of the work was done by anonymous activists in the field who we still do not know and cannot thank to this day.

Soon after the initial uprising, people from Kasserine heard about what was going on in Sidi Bouzid. People in Menzel Bouzayene and Meknassi, two small towns in the Sidi Bouzid state, had relatives in Kasserine. The suffering from unemployment and poverty was even worse in Menzel Bouzayene and Meknassi than it was in Sidi Bouzid center, particularly for their young people. They were tough guys, raised in militant families, and their despair was as big as their anger. The first real battles with the police started in Menzel Bouzayene and Meknassi. Police stations were attacked and burned, police officers were kicked out of town, and the resistance was born.

Tunisian bloggers and cyberactivists did not create a newspaper to cover the events because they already had an electronic one: Nawaat.org. This collective blog founded by Sami Ben Gharbia and Riadh Guerfali in 2004, was already very famous worldwide and affiliated with many human rights and freedom-of-press organizations, especially Reporters Without Borders and Global Voices.

A soon as the uprising started, the blog was used as a hub for all kinds of content. Another platform was Posterous.com, which was useful for two reasons: it could change its address whenever the posters needed to escape Internet censorship, and the site also had a very efficient content management system that allowed posters to publish content simply by sending an e-mail, which was then shared automatically on every social media site already listed in the poster's account: Facebook, Twitter, Digg, Google Buzz, and so on. They also published videos on YouTube, another great advantage since it was censored in Tunisia. Of course, people could get to YouTube through proxies, but uploading the videos could be challenging at best. But we were getting creative and doing everything we could. The whole blogosphere and activist community seemed to share the same feeling, that this was not a "same thing different day" situation; this was the next big thing.

Kasserine was almost in the same state as Sidi Bouzid, and the clash there had begun immediately after Sidi Bouzid's. The videos of riots, demonstrations, and repression that came out of that town made people furious, especially when they heard about the first martyrs. While some average Internet surfers started joining the activists, sharing the news and asking people to help them, a video coming out of Kasserine's hospital brought the whole thing to the next level. It documented many injuries with real bullets and some corpses. One of the victims was shot in the head, and everyone could see his brain coming out. It was graphic and shocking. Rumors started spreading about snipers shooting people in the head and chest. For many of them, it was no longer about social requests or civil rights: it was about vendetta. What had started as a social uprising turned into a war against a regime that showed it had no problem killing its people if they got too noisy.

I was in hell. Nothing was worse for me than seeing all this happen without being able to do anything about it. Though all I wanted was to go out to the street and express my anger, I knew that I had to temper my rage and be smart. My role as a relay for media was much more important than I would be as a single voice screaming alone. I had already attended the December 27 demonstration with many of my friends, and no other calls to action had been made. It was all I could do to wait, watch, and disseminate.

But that graphic and tragic video created a huge buzz in Tunisia and the rest of the world. The well-known blog ReadWriteWeb France, edited by Fabrice Epelboinm and to which I used to contribute, reported on YouTube's attempts to censor the footage—a huge news scoop at the time. However, bloggers at Read Write Web France were not the only foreigners who were deeply involved in this cause. Jillian C. York, an American activist for Global Voices, a citizen media blogging community, and Brian Whitaker, a journalist for *The Guardian* newspaper in London, were following the situation closely and helping us to spread the news and contact international media organizations. Tunisians living outside of the country were active too, uploading and sharing reports and video content and pushing hard to get the international media to cover the uprising. Many Arab bloggers, especially Egyptians, were involved too, through their social media pages, especially the monumental "We are all Khaled Said" Facebook page.

That's when the Anonymous attacks began. I'd known about Anonymous since September 2010, when Slim Amamou introduced the concept to visitors to TEDx Carthage and I interviewed him for Tunivisions about his speech. When I saw Anonymous join the revolutionaries, I knew we had a very strong ally for our cyber war, and it was time to fight.

This *hacktivist* (activist hackers) group published a press release to express its solidarity with the people of Tunisia, and then it started attacking the government and presidential family's companies' Web sites. DDoS (distributed denial of service) attacks made the sites fall offline, while hackers defaced and replaced their homepages with the Operation Payback avatar, the pirate ship of ThePirateBay.org, a Web site of free content-sharing that

Anonymous had previously defended against rights owners who wanted to have it closed.

Tunisians felt a strong sympathy for the movement and started supporting it by sharing its messages and putting its avatar—the Guy Fawkes *V for Vendetta* mask—on their profile pictures.

But the government cyber police decided to join the action. First, they started hacking into accounts on Facebook, replacing the users' profile pictures with the Anonymous picture to make the hacking victims believe Anonymous had perpetrated the hack. The government police then deleted every page for which those users were administrators. The purpose was to decrease the spread of information since, although individual Facebook users cannot have more than five thousand friends, administrators of public pages, previously called "fan pages," have no limit. Some of these public pages had more than six hundred thousand members, which is huge for a country of only 10 million citizens. The government hackers took control of my account and those of many other bloggers, deleting countless pages (Tunivisions lost more than four hundred thousand fans) before we could recover them.

While people were regaining control of their Facebook accounts, Anonymous released a plug-in for them to install on their navigator so the government could not hack them anymore. Meanwhile, many Tunisians had joined the hacktivists' group and gave them support by attacking the government Web sites along with Anonymous and providing a kind of backup hacktivism.

The uprising kept on spreading from town to town, transported by the Internet and by local leaders, especially those from the syndicate UGTT, or General Union of Tunisian Workers, who were organizing, leading, and sometimes even protecting the demonstrations. Their network was very strong, and they had extensive experience in social movements and demonstrations in addition to their popularity among the youth. Meanwhile, the bloggers and cyberactivists became more organized, creating special Facebook pages such as the "News Agency of the Tunisian Street Movement." Nawaat.org recruited many new volunteers to help the team collect data, classify it, and publish it the right way. On December 30, I was invited by Nessma TV to participate in the first TV debate about the events of Sidi Bouzid. That momentous media event broke the blackout about the uprising. The regime wanted to use the debate to temper the people, but the channel decided to go much farther than expected.

By January 6, 2011, the government had decided to put an end to the cyber revolution. Early in the morning, the security of state officers arrested not fewer than nine bloggers, the most famous of whom were Slim Amamou, who later became Secretary of State for Youth and Sports, and Azyz Amami. A big campaign was launched to free them. Concerns about the government hacking into people's accounts even reached the State Department in the United States, thanks to efforts by Facebook's administration. That day, I was lucky. The police came to my parents' house to arrest me, but at the time I was sharing a small house with two friends. My living situation was the only thing that saved me from being arrested, and that arrest attempt forced me to run and hide in some other friends' studio. But it didn't prevent the police from guarding our office for a few days, or from bringing my boss to the interior ministry to ask him "some questions" about me and my colleagues.

The more the movement grew, the worse government censorship became until it reached a point where they were even filtering the secured mode for Facebook. People could not even change their passwords or profile pictures. The purpose was to make us identify ourselves on an unsecured page, so they could sniff out the passwords and take control of the accounts.

When the riots reached the ghettos of Tunis, it was clear that nothing could stop the anger. When I heard that the people of Ettadhamen City and Tahrir were fighting against the police and heading to downtown Tunis, I said to my brother: "Here we are. Ben Ali is done." Neither prisons nor bullets would stop the Tunisian people from fighting against security forces everywhere, especially when they saw that, while the army was not openly supporting the revolt, it was doing nothing to stop it. Calls for demonstrations were made on Facebook, which was also covering the events. Some bloggers, like Slim Amamou, even chose to stream live video with their mobile phones before they got arrested.

On January 13, Ben Ali made a third speech announcing that Internet and media censorship was over and that the detained bloggers had been set free. For the first time since the whole thing started, my fear was that the people would believe him and decide to go back to their homes. If that had happened, we would have suffered the worst revenge. We could not allow it to happen. The lines of communication were wide open, and the syndicate called for a general strike for January 14. Everyone knew that they had to take to the streets to ensure there would be no reforms that would guarantee the sustainability of the regime. Only one outcome was acceptable: Ben Ali had to go.

There I was, in front of the interior ministry with some friends and foreign journalists. People asked me, "How do you feel?" Choking back my tears, I replied, "Simultaneous orgasms of freedom."

We left the avenue by the afternoon and went to the airport to meet an American journalist coming to cover the events. At 5 P.M. the curfew started, and we heard that the Trabelsis, the family of Ben Ali's wife, Leila, had been arrested. I was sitting in the airport café, reading these reports on Twitter from my laptop. When I told other people in the restaurant the news, they shouted, "Long live Tunisia!"

Emotions were even stronger when we heard that Ben Ali had left the country. However, there was no way to celebrate. The curfew was still going on, and we had to spend the night in the airport. My last words on Twitter were to say that Ben Ali was just the big boss but the mafia was still there. If we wanted to be free, we had to dissolve his party, the RCD. I called for a big demonstration, just like the one we'd had earlier that day, in front of the local RCD. That demonstration occurred a few days later. There was no stopping us now.

SYRIA

OVERVIEW

Syria often seemed like the last country in the world that would have a peaceful, secular revolution. Few countries have a leadership based so strongly on a personality cult. Bashar al-Assad, the current president, has ruled for twelve long years. His father, Hafez al-Assad, preceded him with a twenty-nine-year run. Portraits of the two plaster public spaces throughout the country. From 1963 to 2011 an official state of emergency meant that the constitution and the rights it protected were a mirage. Syrian prisons are legendary, as is the country's network of secret police and informants, which in its level of penetration resembles the Stasi of East Germany. The machinations of the Assad family and their associates would be at home in a Mario Puzo novel: brutal, strategic, and opaque.

What the government didn't manipulate with fear, it controlled with a grudging respect, bolstered, of course, by robust propaganda. As little breathing room as the Assad dynasty gave its people politically, living in Syria was often comparably better than in almost every neighboring country. When Syrians thought of change, they looked to Lebanon and saw intractable civil war. In Iraq they saw the even more brutal and much more arbitrary rule of Saddam Hussein, and later a terrifying occupation and civil war. In Palestine they saw a people dispossessed by foreigners, and in the Arabian

Peninsula they saw religious fundamentalism that many found distasteful. The ruling Syrian Baath Party has a secular, pan-Arab agenda, and the Assads are from a minority sect, the Allawites, that some conservative Sunnis regard as heretics. This made some of Syria's many religious and ethnic minorities—among them some 1.5 million Christians—prefer the flawed regime over the possibility of a tyranny of the majority in the form of a conservative Sunni state. Some still do. Indeed, Hafez al-Assad brutally crushed religious extremism in the 1980s, and it never really returned. Finally, while Syria was never a rich country, its command economy and socialist underpinnings mean that profound poverty has been unusual. All of this meant that, while there was little love lost for a regime that almost everyone knew was brutal, the variables, when added together, just couldn't add up to revolution.

That, at least, was what many experts thought. But in 2011, the Syrian people proved them wrong. Maybe it was the country's long tradition of intellectual vibrancy, which dates back to the eras when Damascus was a major Roman, Byzantine, and then Islamic cultural capital. Maybe it was the satellite TV that began to beam into people's homes in the early 2000s, through dishes that cluttered the rooftops of the cities like so many hungry birds looking to the sky. The Internet definitely played a role, connecting dissidents in the huge Syrian diaspora with free thinkers in the country. Or it could have been the rapid economic liberalization that Bashar al-Assad promoted, which some said introduced a new inequality and the experience of serious poverty. Probably, as in so many Arab countries, the revolution had to do with dignity and pride, for Syrians certainly love their country.

Whatever it was, something had changed in the Syrian equation, and when the breezes of the Arab Spring wafted down the Mediterranean Coast, the Syrian revolt blossomed.

It began in the southern city of Dera'a in late January 2011. Although the protests were at first limited to that city, the government's brutal crackdown actually spurred them onward elsewhere.

The most famous incident was the killing of Hamza al-Khatib, thirteen, presumably at the hands of the secret police, for writing anti-government graffiti. When pictures of his severely mutilated body made the rounds on the Internet, it rallied the Syrian people throughout the country. Soon almost every city, particularly Hama and Homs in the Orontes Valley, had weekly mass demonstrations calling for the downfall of the regime, greater freedoms, and the end of Baath rule.

The uprising has been down a rocky road and faces many more obstacles in the future. The government has made some small reforms—for instance, Assad lifted the emergency law in April 2011. But the crackdown only grew more brutal. By year's end, more than five thousand Syrians were dead, and tens of thousands had been arrested. While the protests were overwhelmingly peaceful at first, some had taken on a militant tone—partly because some members of the army defected, but also because some groups advocated violent takeover. While many Syrians remain firmly supportive of the protests, others, especially minorities, are more frightened than ever about what chaos might come next. The United Nations has said the country may be near civil war. A deadly car bomb in Damascus in December, and worsening violence throughout the country, has bolstered these fears.

What has changed irrevocably is that, for the first time in decades, the question of Syria's political future is one about which its people have expressed their opinions. Even as the protests' specific legacy remains unknown, it is clear that Syria has entered a new era.

PATRIOT AND FUGITIVE

Razan Zaitouneh

Razan Zaitouneh, thirty-four, is a Syrian human rights lawyer who has been a member of the team defending political prisoners since 2001. In that year, she was one of the founders of the Human Rights Association in Syria (HRAS). In 2005, she established SHRIL (the Syrian Human Rights Information Link), through which she continues to report about human rights violations in Syria. Since 2005, Razan has been an active member of the Committee to Support Families of Political Prisoners in Syria.

Portions of this essay previously appeared in a slightly different form on the Web site The Damascus Bureau.

My participation in the street protests the Syrian people began in March could not last long. My willingness to share information with foreign journalists caught up with me quickly. It was only a few weeks after the protests began in the southern part of the country when I realized I would need to go into hiding or face arrest. From what I knew about prison conditions in Syria, I of course wanted to avoid that—but that wasn't my only reason for not wanting to go to jail. The moment for which many Syrians had been waiting for so long was finally at hand: a mass, peaceful movement, uniting diverse communities, calling for the end of a regime that no one had elected. I needed to continue the fight. To do that, I had to hide. I write this now from a location I cannot disclose, to try to spread the word of my fellow citizens who are risking their lives to save their country.

Syrians began protesting in small numbers as early as January 2011. They were inspired by Tunisia and Egypt, which showed that even the most daunting dictators could be toppled. As a human rights lawyer based in Damascus who usually represented political prisoners, I was excited about the possibility of change in Syria. I was tired of the arbitrary power of the security forces and the long suspension of our rights under the emergency laws.

Foreign journalists were strictly prohibited from working in Syria. The government was trying to make an airtight information seal around the country so that they could spread their propaganda and create doubt about the peaceful aims of the protesters. This was an area where I knew I could help the protesters. I started to publish the latest news on my Facebook page and called the international media myself, to send them the news and ask them to pay attention to what was going on. After a while, I started to work in a more organized way with other activists in a Skype group to send the news and translate it. We managed to get eyewitness accounts to the media.

By March, the protests had developed into a full-scale uprising in the southern governorate of Dera'a. After confrontations with the police, protesters had retreated to the Omari mosque in the city of Dera'a. On March 23, security forces surrounded the mosque and brutally attacked it. In the massacre that followed, many more than one hundred unarmed protesters were killed. I wasn't there, but I was able to gather information from Dera'a and pass it on to international media.

I was not so surprised when, shortly thereafter, Syrian state television declared that I was a foreign agent. I knew I was in danger and that the security forces would come to get me soon. I packed a few necessities and left my apartment.

The security forces waited a few weeks. On April 30, they raided my home and found nobody but my brother-in-law, 'Abd-al-Rahman Al-Hamada. So they arrested him as a hostage. Then on May 11, they arrested my husband, Wa'il Al-Hamada. He was imprisoned for almost three months—where, I don't know—during which time he was tortured and not allowed to communicate with the outside world. I believe that my husband and his brother were held to try to force me to turn myself in.

Of course, I am not a foreign agent but a patriot who loves her country. That is why I continued my work in secret. I have managed to keep my contacts with activists, and reported the stories of brave Syrians facing danger for their nation. In sharing these stories with the world, I hope to advance the cause of these visionaries and fight the propaganda that has still kept some Syrians from joining the uprising. Here are two of those stories.

MOHAMMED

Mohammed is a man from Dera'a in his early twenties. Whenever I meet protesters, especially from this city where the revolution began, I like to ask how they overcame the fear, faced the monster of aggressive repression, and ventured into the streets. I think the psychological barrier to action in Syria is something that might be hard for foreigners to understand.

Mohammed's memories of the first demonstration that took place in Jiza, a city in Dera'a governorate, shed some light on that moment.

"The number of participants was low, maybe one hundred fifty," he recalled. "We came out very spontaneously and stayed about two hours in the demonstration in the hope that more people would join us. But in the end we were not more than four hundred people. The chanting [at that time] was that people wanted to reform the regime.

"It was the first time in my life that I spoke this way. I felt fear, so we did not speak up much during the chanting. But I also felt that I heard my voice for the first time. After the demonstration ended, we could not believe what we had done. In fact, even today I cannot believe the situation we are in now, when ten people became a hundred, and those became a thousand, the sound gradually became higher and chants were rising."

As Mohammed remembers it, the start of the demonstrations was completely spontaneous. On hearing the news of what was happening in Dera'a, young men poured into the streets. But after a while, things became more organized. A group of young people took charge of coordinating the protests of Jiza.

For several months, the army and security forces surrounded Jiza, like other areas of Dera'a. Day and night they raided houses— either of activists in the demonstrations or random houses in order to intimidate people. They brutally detained people, stole, and looted.

"But the most provocative of all for us," Mohammed said, "was the message left by the elements of the regime at the end of this party of repression. Throughout the town they had written on the walls slogans such as 'You're the disease and we are the medicine. If you come back [to protest] we will come back. And our return will be tough. No god but Bashar.'"

Once the military had left, the task of the youth of Jiza would be to replace those words with phrases like, "Syria is free. Leave, Bashar. We are waiting."

Not all of the interactions with the army were bad—and therein lay some hope. Maybe it had something to do with the fact that many of the soldiers are young conscripts of humble backgrounds.

"Many of them were respectful and easy to deal with because they sympathized with us," Mohammed said. "But they could not do anything. Whoever refuses to obey orders would be executed. Some of them when they took our identities at the checkpoints apologized and asked us to forgive them. And we forgive them. But others we don't even consider as Syrians anymore because of their violence and abusive words toward us."

Despite the siege and ongoing raids, mass demonstrations in Jiza continued.

"I didn't care about dying," Mohammed said, adding that in fact he often despised himself for staying alive when he saw loved ones and friends shot dead by security forces.

When towns and villages came out to lift the siege of the city of Dera'a on April 29, "the wounded were my brothers and my neighbors and my friends. It was the only time I cried in my life. I cried until I almost collapsed," he recalled.

Since then in Jiza, as in other places, the idea of a militarization of the revolution has started to enter the minds of some young people. "We began peaceful and we want peace until the end," Mohammed said. "But after every massacre, you hear voices that consider militarization the only solution to stop the massacres. How long can we bear the crimes that are happening?" he wondered.

He recalled the effect of witnessing a massacre. "Dozens of wounded, dead around you, blood, pain everywhere, and people dying in your arms—whoever had to witness such moments naturally thinks about getting armed," he said. "And not all people are university graduates or educated. But we know that no weapon would have been enough to face the tanks [of the army] so those ideas vanished quickly."

YAHYA AND THE ROSES

Many protesters had the same realization as Mohammed: an armed resistance against Syrian forces would not work for a variety of reasons, but especially because any attempt would be vastly outgunned.

In Deraya, a suburb of Damascus that has been an eager participant in the protests, a group of young people have pioneered a novel form of resistance: roses.

Yahya is a member of the Coordination Committee of Daraya, an activist group, who described to me the meetings with activists that led them to decide on their tactic. He explained to me that some youths in the community wanted to greet the army with stones, but through discussion they became convinced that such a confrontation would be futile. Worse, it would play into the hands of what the regime wanted—the appearance of a civil war and a justification for counterviolence. Yahya and his colleagues even tried to avoid using terms that imply violent struggle, such as the word *rebels* (*thuwar*) used in the case of Libya. Rather, they insisted on using the phrase "the youth of the revolution" (*shabab al-thawra*), based on the Egyptian model. There were also questions raised of whether throwing stones and burning tires in symbolic protest would be against the nonviolent character of the movement. Despite the fact that such practices do not literally conflict with the nonviolence of the revolution, Yahya is strongly against them. He considers them to be provocations against low-ranking soldiers, most of whom are under twenty years old and doing mandatory military service under constant investigation by their ranking officers and in isolation from their families and home communities for several months. When these soldiers see smoke and fire, they feel that they are in a battle and must play a battle role.

What the protesters decided on was roses—one rose for every protester. The idea took off, and some of the youths who had been the most enthusiastic about stone throwing came up with the idea to distribute water and roses to security personnel during the summer.

The idea was put into practice when huge numbers of military and security personnel surrounded the area where protests normally occur. The protesters gathered near them and started lining up water bottles and roses in the no-man's-land between the two groups. Attached were leaflets that said, "We are all Syrians. Why are you killing us?"

In response, the soldiers began releasing tear gas and shooting rubber bullets, and the protesters stepped back a few feet. A young man named Islam al-Dabbas took on the role of delivering the message. He came near the row of water bottles and roses and began speaking to the security and military personnel about the peacefulness of the revolution and its goals, which include inflicting no harm on soldiers or anyone else.

The soldiers were puzzled at first. Then they began collecting and reading the leaflets that the protesters had cast their way. As they did, protesters chanted, "The army and the people, hand in hand." Then the soldiers began gathering the water bottles off the ground. One of them tried to shoot rubber bullets at the protest again, but his colleagues prevented him from doing so; indeed, they were waving at the protesters, who quietly walked away.

It's not as if this magically stopped the crackdown. The following Friday, Islam insisted on crossing the dividing line and offering roses to the soldiers and security personnel directly. He aimed to achieve a kind of eye-to-eye connection between the protesters and those who had come to kill and suppress them. This kind of encounter breaks psychological barriers and allows the other side to see what the regime's lies and propaganda prevent them from seeing. Such an encounter is usually difficult to achieve considering that orders to shoot are often timed so that soldiers fire from a distance, and hence have no interaction with the protesters except by way of weapons. Islam disappeared among the security personnel, who seized him and the roses that he had sought to offer them. He remains in a cell to this day, held by the secret police.

But such scenes are ones that at least some of the protesters are willing to accept. Similar tactics of offering gifts to the army have been adopted at many other rallies since.

The rose revolutionaries hope that they can change more than just the regime. While many Syrian activists have embraced nonviolence as a tactic, fewer have embraced it as a principle. Yahya, forever the idealist, hopes for a double revolution—a political one and a revolution of the mentality of Syrians. He thinks he sees it slowly taking shape. Young Syrians, he thinks, are now waking to the possibilities of democracy and civil rights—and maybe even nonviolence as a principle.

It is a big dream. But it is the dreamers who are doing the impossible in Syria today.

BAHRAIN

OVERVIEW

In the West, Bahrain's 2011 uprising is perhaps the least known of all the movements of the Arab Spring. The island nation of 1.2 million in the Persian Gulf made headlines briefly in the spring, but then—as far as most of the world was concerned, anyway—seemed to quiet down.

But Bahrain is not quiet at all. Moreover, the causes and outcomes of the tumult there involve major powers, sectarianism, debates about the virtue of revolution versus reform, and a peek into the limits of American support for the Arab Spring. Bahrain is an intersection for issues that have reverberations around the Middle East.

The country, a constitutional monarchy headed by King Hamad bin Isa Al-Khalifa, is connected to the Kingdom of Saudi Arabia by a sixteen-mile bridge, the King Fahd causeway. Bahrain is often known to expats living in Saudi Arabia as the closest place with a relatively more permissive atmosphere. This is partly due to Bahrain's history—having long been a strategic way station on the routes between India, Persia, and the Arab world, it gained an increasingly diverse character over the years. Before the Al-Khalifa family gained control of it in 1783, the island was a Persian holding. Today, a majority of the population is Shia, which is also the dominant Islamic sect in Iran. There is also a population of Christians, and until the 1940s there was a significant Jewish population as well. Like most Gulf countries, Bahrain has large numbers of migrant workers, hailing especially from South Asia and the Philippines. But even among Bahraini citizens, people trace diverse ancestries, not necessarily dependent on their religion. There are Bahrainis of Arab, Persian, and East African descent, to name a few.

The ruling family, however, is not so diverse. The Khalifa family is Sunni Arab with close ties to Saudi Arabia. Bahraini activists assert that the Sunni minority, and particularly those connected to the royal family, enjoy a position of privilege in society. Worse, they complain that the Shia are repressed, even persecuted.

Abroad, this situation is often described as a sectarian conflict. This is only partly true. Religious identity is an issue in Bahrain mostly because of the way it has been tied up in politics and well-being, not because of doctrinal disputes. Shia are well represented in parliament, but the parliament has relatively little power. (That parliamentarians were arrested and tortured in the wake of the 2011 protests painfully drove this point home.) As a result, the Shia have little power relative to their share of the population. They are also relatively economically disadvantaged. Directly fueling the ire of the protesters this year were allegations—substantiated by Google Earth and circulated by e-mail after the government blocked that program—that the royal family is hoarding land while most Bahrainis live in relatively cramped, unaffordable housing. The inequities have given rise to protests before, most notably in the 1990s. After some steps toward more power sharing and constitutional rule in the 2000s, the country backslid. By the time of parliamentary elections of 2010, which many opposition parties boycotted, there was growing discontent in Bahrain.

Then came Tunisia, and like so many people in the region, Bahrainis took to the streets. It was now a proven fact that difficult change could be effected through mass action. Organized by some of the opposition parties, protesters occupied Pearl Roundabout for weeks in February. There were clashes with police, but the protesters stood their ground and caught the world's attention. At the beginning, they were calling not for outright revolution but for serious reform. The main established political opposition party, Al-Wefaq, continues calling for reform, but many youth protesters, hardened after months of repression, are clamoring for revolution.

But the euphoric resistance was short-lived. The government called in its allies in Saudi Arabia, who had the firepower to put down the insurrection, which they did, under the auspices of the Gulf Cooperation Council, with noted brutality. More than forty Bahrainis were killed during the protests, and thousands were arrested, many tortured. This led some protesters to change their focus from reform to an end of the monarchy. Police cleared the Pearl Roundabout, and the government declared martial law. Bahrain receded from the headlines and the most urgent parts of the Western diplomatic agenda.

The reason for that last point is not just Bahrain's small size. The country enjoys an extremely close relationship with the United States. It is a major non-NATO ally (MNNA) and hosts the U.S. Navy's strategically critical Fifth Fleet. It is also a place where the United States seeks to counter Iranian influence in the region, something it is nervous about, considering Bahrain's historic ties to Persia. All of this has led to many speculations that the Americans have been soft on the regime there, heaping praise on it for being a regional leader of openness, even as NGOs have noted that the political environment and human rights situation were deteriorating.

The protesters may lament this American support of the monarchy, but their concerns are not geopolitical: they want equal rights and justice, economic opportunity and—like so many marchers in the Arab Spring—dignity.

A BUMPY ROAD WITH NO ALTERNATIVE:
Q&A WITH MATAR IBRAHIM MATAR

Matar Ibrahim Matar is a former member of parliament in Bahrain and a prominent member of Al-Wefaq National Islamic Society, which is the largest single political party in Bahrain and the leader of the opposition. Despite having been tortured and kept in solitary confinement for forty-five days earlier this year for his role in the protests, he continues to believe that reform—not revolution—is the best way to ensure civil rights for his constituents. He answered our questions by e-mail in the days after the Bahrain Independent Commission of Inquiry released its controversial report about the treatment of prisoners in the country.

You *studied in Kuwait before returning to Bahrain, where you swiftly rose to prominence in Al-Wefaq. How did you get involved in politics?*

While I was in Kuwait in 1994, there was an uprising in Bahrain, and I got excited about being in politics. But there was no space to express even our sympathy with the movement in Bahrain. Still, I had become very interested in the youth and student activities that were taking place, and I had a growing interest in political Islam. It was an exciting period with a lot of debates.

When I returned to Bahrain in 2002, I established the Bahrain Youth Center, which was part of Al-Wefaq.[14] At that time I presented to the center a book, *The Theories of State in the Shiite Jurisprudence*, by an Iranian philosopher, Mohsen Kadivar. Kadivar had been arrested in Iran for his thoughts and political activities. He is a dissident and a critic of the official opinion on the source of legitimacy in Islam in the country. By presenting his book, I was declaring my thoughts about political Islam, which I believe doesn't contradict liberty and democracy. I was worried how such ideas would be received among other youth, but later I discovered that such ideas represent the norm in Bahrain and inside Al-Wefaq.

The Bahrain Youth Center was the only youth group in the country that was regularly represented by new faces. It was one of our rules that one could not be a leader of this center for more than two years. In a small country such as Bahrain, it was difficult to implement such a rule, but we insisted on having it so that nobody hijacked the environment or the movement. I'm happy to see that this rule is still implemented, even though it means I have lost the ability to interfere in the project that I established!

Before the opposition was divided into Al-Wefaq and Haq,[15] leaders on both sides nominated me to be in the Consultative Council of Al-Wefaq. Later I was elected by the Al-Wefaq Assembly, which set the strategies, approved the policy, and monitored the implementation of the Al-Wefaq Secretariat.

In the honoring ceremony for the sponsors and volunteers who were supporting Al-Wefaq, General Secretary of Al-Wefaq Sheik Ali Salman introduced me to the audience as his replacement in the next election. I was a relative unknown then, and I know many people asked themselves the questions "Who is Matar?" and "Why Matar?" As I spoke to the audience that day, I tried to focus on setting a realistic expectation about what I could add in the complex situation in the country. Bahrainis are not too hopeful about the result of Al-Wefaq's contribution because they all have the clear idea that our parliament is part of a fake democracy. Most resort to harsh criticisms of the regime, or just make fun of the stupid justifications it makes for the corruption and the violations. But I clearly made it known from the beginning that I don't have such skills—I'm not one for giving heavy speeches. I think people were a little unhappy when they heard me say this, but maybe by now they are happy with Al-Wefaq's decision.

What changed this year (2011) in Bahrain, or for Bahrainis, that made mass action a possibility?

Maybe it was strange to have such a movement in an oil-producing country in the middle of the Gulf.[16] It is also strange to see such a movement in one of the United States' MNNAs. The U.S. State Department has marketed Bahrain as a leading model in the region. When I asked Secretary of State Hillary Clinton about United States–Bahrain relations during the Manama Dialogue in 2010,[17] she said, "Changes that are happening in Bahrain are much greater than what I see in many other countries in the region and beyond." How could such a place experience such turmoil?

The reality is that Bahrain is facing deep economic and social problems. There is a major housing problem because there has been a merger between public ownership and the ruling family's private ownership. The total value of all public properties that have been transferred to private ownership is about $50 billion. At the same time, Bahrain is providing a lot of facilities to external investors to cover for its failure to motivate its own private sector to create new jobs. This policy has led to a tremendous jump in the prices of properties for which the only beneficiaries are influential people, not the economy of Bahrain.

The regime is proud because our economy ranks higher than that of the United Kingdom in economic freedom indicators, but Bahrainis themselves are not free. Currently, even some upper-middle-class people are unable to own houses in Bahrain.

In addition to these economic problems, there is a systematic discrimination policy against Shia, and antigovernment opinions in general. This policy has sometimes reached the level of persecution, which is a type of crime against humanity, according to the Rome Statute of the International Criminal Court.

It is worth mentioning that Bahrain has been regressing after earlier progress. In 2001 all political prisoners were released and all exiled activists were allowed to return. But then things started getting bad again. The comprehensive Human Rights Watch report *Torture Redux*,[18] which was released before the Arab Spring, gives a good picture of what has happened. Bahrain has slid in Freedom House's rankings from being a "partially free" country to being a "non-free" country. *The Economist* has also called the Bahraini regime "authoritarian." We have declined in our ratings in the Transparency International Report. All these declines happened before the uprising, but the international community ignored them, and the Bahraini regime was called a "major strategic ally" and close friend to the West. Tension increased in 2010 with the imprisonment of activists on terrorism charges.[19] Taken together, these signals indicate in hindsight that the political temperature in Bahrain at the start of 2011 was about to a reach boiling point when Mohammed Bouazizi set himself on fire in Tunisia to protest the economic discrimination suffered by working-class people in the Arab world. In doing so, he touched a chord with people all over the region who have seen their autocratic leaders enrich themselves at the expense of political and social reforms.

What were the demands of the uprising?

Simply put, the people want to share the power and wealth with the ruling family, but the monarchy is refusing. It's no surprise that they refuse. If I was in their position of privilege, with their mentality, I might refuse, too. But in the twenty-first century, no one should accept or make excuses for feudalism. It is the right of

Bahrainis, and the people are insisting on having it, regardless of whether it is a feasible goal or not and regardless of whether the West calls the regime authoritarian or a strategic ally. Right now, Bahrainis are drunk with the slogans of liberty and democracy, but they are also seriously committed to seeing tangible results on the ground.

This is a movement of dignity. Many activists have good jobs and good living standards, but they are refusing to be slaves for this regime. They would like to move forward, to live in a state instead of living in a tribe. Bahrainis are insisting on having an elected government, a full legislative council that has real authority, and an independent and fair judiciary system. Our demands are really very basic, and they pertain to universal rights.

What are the big differences and similarities between the movement in Bahrain and those in other Arab countries, especially Egypt and Tunisia?

There are many similarities in terms of demands, but there are huge differences in terms of the circumstances.

When it came to the reaction from Saudi Arabia, I think the timing was also critical. The Saudis failed to help Mubarak or Ben Ali, and this turned Bahrain into a battle of revenge for them. So Saudi Arabia helped put down Bahrain's revolt, even though I don't believe that what's happening in Bahrain could really affect the stability of the Saudi regime the way Egypt might.

In addition to this, Bahrain may not have the same poverty that exists in Egypt and Tunisia. But when you look at the cost of living in the Persian Gulf, especially the price of property, I believe we have other kinds of living difficulties.

What do you think of the idea that Bahrain is a location for contests to be played out between Saudi Arabia and Iran?

Bahrain has a unique and complex geopolitical position since it is in between Iran and Saudi Arabia, and since it hosts the U.S.

Navy's Fifth Fleet. So Bahrain became a battlefield between Saudi Arabia and Iran.

I'm not happy to see this, nor to see Bahrain become the icon of persecution against Shia in the region. Such designations make the solution to our political problems much more complicated than it should be because we are in a region with a complicated sectarian issue. And the government utilizes the regional conflict to refuse change. They are always lamenting the sectarian polarization here, and yet it is they who made it.

This year (2011), you were imprisoned, tortured, and kept in solitary confinement for forty-five days for your political activities. Can you tell us about that—the charges, the trial, and your arrest?

Before my imprisonment, I was representing the largest constituency in Bahrain. I got about 85 percent of the votes in the 2010 elections, which was one of the largest votes and percentages. I believe that my torture and ill treatment following the protests this spring was degrading for Bahrainis and for their choices.

The charges against me were fake, trumped up to exact revenge against Al-Wefaq for the role it had played in the protest. I consider myself a hostage taken to put pressure on my party to stop demanding real political reform. The Bahrain Independent Commission of Inquiry (BICI), which issued its final report in late November 2011, mentioned my case as an example of ill treatment.[20]

The most difficult part of the ordeal was the interrogations, when I wasn't allowed to sleep. I suffered from depression, and I wasn't able to eat or rest properly. When you hear the sound of torture in the prison, usually you expect the worst. This expectation is sometimes much harder than the torture itself.

Of course I cannot generalize because many torture cases led to death during the last unrest. Thank God I wasn't in that position.

I was physically tortured by someone who was called "Sheik," which is the title of members of the ruling family. I sent complaints about this incident to the Royal Court. I was expecting for them to deal seriously with my letter, but it was totally ignored, and I didn't get a reply. A similar letter was sent to the general prosecutor asking him to investigate this issue, but he didn't reply.

Right now, however, my trial has been suspended. The BICI report recommended that all torture complaints should be processed,[21] a recommendation that has been heeded, so my trial will not begin until the investigation of the ill treatment is finished. Further, my charges are related to offenses involving political expression. The BICI report said that such charges should be reviewed or dropped,[22] but the judge has refused to take this step, and there has still been no investigation about the ill treatment.

Despite the threats I'm facing, I'm in a better position now. Before, it was possible that I might be sentenced very harshly because of my initial, fabricated charges. One man detained after the uprisings, Ali Saqer, appeared on state television and said I ordered him to kill security forces by running over them with his car. Saqer later died in custody; the signs of torture were clear on his body. After his death, it seemed that Bahrain Intelligence decided to reduce my charges because they knew nobody would believe them. My current charges are contributing to the Arab Spring demonstration in Bahrain and giving false rumors to the media.

Despite this terrible experience, you are still hopeful that Bahrain can be improved through reform, not revolution. Can you explain why you think this is possible?

Many Bahrainis don't have hope that the current regime can be reformed. They argue with us in Al-Wefaq: if this regime refuses to accept reform, why don't we support overthrow of the regime?

Yes, it is true that we are in a difficult situation whenever the regime rejects change, and it is not easy for us to convince anyone that there is hope. But I believe that overthrowing the regime is not feasible for a lot of reasons, even if the West changes its tone and starts to call Bahrain an authoritarian regime instead of a strategic ally. We will still face a deep problem with our neighbor, Saudi

Arabia. We cannot think about a change that bypasses the situation in Saudi Arabia—our economy is very much linked to them, even dependent. I believe that a democracy with regional isolation is not viable. We in Al-Wefaq have a deep belief in working with regional circumstances, which we also want to change. Simply put, there is no future for Bahrain without regional reform, and no future for Bahrain without strong relations with the Saudis and the West. And there is a conflict between those two goals. We hope we may have an exit from this complicated situation. In the end, I think there is a margin for maneuvering. The excessive force exercised in response to the uprisings actually caused many troubles for the West and the Saudis. All sides are thinking about alternative ways to realize their interests in a way that is least damaging to their credibility.

Do you think the uprisings have been successful? What has changed as a result of the uprisings? What have you learned?

Day after day the number of demonstrators is increasing.[23] The people are not afraid anymore of the excessive force used by riot police, though we are worried about the safety of the demonstrators. More victims have lost their lives and been permanently disabled, even as the BICI continued its work.

We haven't reached our goal yet. After all the evidence about the systematic crimes that happened during the unrest—they may reach the level of crimes against humanity—the government is still in power. Nobody in the international community asks the Bahraini prime minister to step down as they have with Bashar Al-Assad in Syria. The regime is still close friends with the West.

By excessive force, the regime succeed in suppressing the uprising. In this small country of Bahrain, there were 45 killings, 1,500 cases of arbitrary arrest, 1,866 cases of torture and ill treatment, 500 prisoners of conscience, destruction of 40 places of worship, 2,710 summary sackings, 500 people in exile, 3 men on death row, and 477 students expelled.[24] Amnesty International summarized the situation by calling Bahrainis bloodied but unbowed.[25]

What is your opinion of the report of the BICI?

In Al-Wefaq we believe that the BICI report contains clear information that documents the claims made by pro-democracy opposition groups, international media, and NGOs of a repressive and dictatorial regime in Bahrain that reacted disproportionately and illegally to legitimate demands of democracy and civil rights. If the western countries do not fulfill their obligation to Bahrain as a major strategic ally, and with no remedy to our grievances, the situation in Bahrain will continue to deteriorate. The population is segregated, repressed, and desperate. The BICI recommendations offer a chance to take a first step toward preventing the escalation of violence and the loss of life, and to eventually build a fair political system, which is the only guarantee of durable stability in Bahrain and the whole region. With the BICI reports as background, the international community will need to take a definite side. It can and should support the democracy fighters in Bahrain, who have been brutally repressed by their regime. Of course, it can also continue covering for this authoritarian regime and accepting its maneuvering while hypocritically advising the opposition to endlessly compromise and resign the enjoyment of our legitimate rights of democracy and the rule of law.

What are your hopes for the future of your country?

I always believed that change in Bahrain is not a threat for the Saudis or the West. I would like to see the Saudis and West competing with Iran to see who can be the most supportive of change, rather than just remaining afraid of the future. The secular democracy, not the theocratic one, is our preferable model, and I'm hopeful that the West and the Saudis will not be too late in seeing this, too.

Ultimately, the best path for us is to reach change with the king himself participating, without external pressure. I support a constructive path, communicating with the Saudis and the Bahraini regime. But they are not willing to talk at the moment, and people are angry about the regime's systematic crimes.

That leaves me in the middle—I may lose my credibility with the people or be punished again by the regime. It is a bumpy road, but there are no alternatives.

DARKNESS BEFORE DAWN

Ala'a Shehabi

Dr. Ala'a Shehabi is an economics lecturer, activist, and writer in Bahrain and a former policy analyst at the RAND Corporation. Her husband has been jailed since April 12 for allegedly participating in the Bahrain protests of 2011.

FEBRUARY 14: DAY OF RAGE IN BAHRAIN

We were glued to the screen on February 11 to watch the announcement of the end of Mubarak's reign. That was when many Bahrainis, including myself, decided to heed the February 14 call for a "Day of Rage." There is no doubt that the Arab Spring effect spilled over directly into Bahrain because we had just seen the impossible happen. Mubarak fell, and what the Egyptians managed to do we could do as well, couldn't we? Every time another country rises, and another dictator falls, I can still physically feel the resurgence of revolutionary zeal pump through my veins.

The winds of democracy had finally reached the shores of the Arab world. The authoritarianism that had been sustained for decades depended on fear and involuntary servitude. Now the fear had gone, and people in Bahrain faced tanks and bullets with bare chests. I therefore did not falter a moment in my decision to take part in the uprising on February 14.

It was either now or never. I held the firm conviction that the time had come. Bahrainis no longer wanted to be "subjects of the King." They wanted to be considered citizens by the state. Even a handout payment of nearly $3,000 the day before did not stop people from going to the street on February 14. We occupied the Pearl Roundabout after the funeral of Ali Mushaimi nearby on February 15. I worked hard for a month in the encampment at the Pearl Roundabout.

Before that, I had shied away from direct political activism and worked as a researcher and economics lecturer. Politics were always trouble in this part of the world, and the youth my age were interested in other things: becoming successful bankers, traveling to Europe. Very few young people appeared to be concerned or active in politics. My small circle of friends would meet every week and complain but felt they could not do much.

But now people, including myself, have completely changed. Every minute of the day, I think about what I need to be doing next to sustain the battle to gain freedom, not just for my husband but for myself and for others. None of us are free. We have been living off the whim of an autocrat who decided our fate with a stroke of the pen. Because of this, there have been cyclical uprisings in Bahrain since the 1930s. This one (in 2011) was the biggest in history, and I prayed that it would be the last one so that our children could live in a better world.

The dream wasn't to last long. For each one of us who found our freedom at the Pearl Roundabout, we felt heart-wrenching pain as we watched the Pearl monument be destroyed in mid-March.[26] What Bahrainis have proven is that such a spirit cannot be crushed with brute force.

It was difficult for me initially facing the fear of repression, death, the pre-dawn raids, the mass arrests, and the sectarian persecution. I had lived a fairly sanitized life up until this point.

PUNISHMENT BY PROXY: MY HUSBAND'S ARREST

My husband Ghazi was not an activist, but I had become one on February 14. He would joke that he had never carried a placard in his life, and I would look at him with disdain, but other times I would envy his nonchalance, given the seemingly hopeless state of the Arab world and the disillusionment of many people at the time. When the uprising began, he preferred to stay at home and look after the baby, and he told me to "go do [my] thing." This was a great deal as far as I was concerned: I could devote myself from February 14 onwards to the *intifada*[27] that was unfolding.

On April 12, we had lunch at home as usual. Ghazi played with our newborn baby and then drove back to his office, where he works as a property executive in one of the biggest commercial companies in Bahrain. I did not hear from him again that day, and his phone was switched off. That evening, the notorious *mukhabarat*[28] Twitter account called Hareghum tweeted, "Ghazi Farhan the traitor has been successfully arrested." This news was a total shock. I feared for my baby as I expected police to raid the house at any moment. Ghazi was the last person I imagined to get arrested.

I later found out from his colleagues at work that Ghazi was followed into his office car park by three SUVs, and men in street clothes—not uniforms—accosted him in the parking lot of his building. They blindfolded and handcuffed him and took him away. This was the notorious National Security Agency, the *mukhabarat*. He endured five days of torture during interrogation and was forced to sign a confession. The officers would call him "Shehabi" (my name, not his), and many of the questions were about me. The last line of the confession (which I have recently obtained) reads, "I have advised my wife many times to stop all political activity." It was clear as day that the point of his arrest was to punish and to silence me.

It wasn't until forty-eight days after his arrest that he emerged alive, but only to be summoned before a military tribunal, which sentenced him to three years in prison following a ten-minute hearing. His two charges were "participating in an illegal assembly of more than five persons," based on the fact that he had visited the Pearl Roundabout, where the protests were centered, and "spreading false information on the Internet," based on a single comment he made on Facebook. He has remained in jail since.

The first glimpse I had of my husband during this time was when he appeared at the military tribunal. It was a terrible sight. He was exhausted, with bloodshot eyes and red marks on his wrists from being handcuffed overnight. I guessed he had lost about twenty pounds. He also looked disoriented, and I can only imagine how shocking it was for him to find himself in a courtroom after such a long time and to be read his charges by three stern judges—serious charges, which he was hearing for the first time—and told to state his plea. And he did all of this while trying to overcome the emotions of seeing his loved ones sitting on benches at the back of the courtroom for the first time in nearly seven weeks. "Is this my husband?" I thought. The man who usually dressed in expensive suits, who drove fast cars and had the airs and graces of a "high-flyer" was in a gray prisoner jumpsuit trying hard to compose himself. The intention was to degrade and punish him.

For months, I was unable to communicate regularly with Ghazi as he was moved around from prison to prison. But on further meetings at the court and on the phone, I saw a new man. The transformation in him was astounding and captures the essence of the Arab Awakening—that it is fundamentally about dignity, not politics. Ghazi refused to be broken or to appear broken. He stood tall, would sneak in a wink, and would express more worry over me than for himself. He was taking the bullet on my behalf, and I am eternally grateful to him.

It's important to remember that there are five hundred other political prisoners in a similar or worse predicament than Ghazi and who remain in jail, out of a total of nearly three thousand arrested over a two-month period. My husband tells me he has been "spoilt" relative to others with him who faced much more severe torture and sentences of up to life imprisonment. Part of why I am so outspoken about his ordeal is that this is not just a personal issue—it's a national tragedy.

I found my personal ordeal very painful, particularly with a newborn baby, and I had to find a way to either detach or deal with the pain so that it didn't paralyze me. After my husband's arrest, I had to decide: Do I continue activism at further risk to myself, or do I stay at home to look after the baby? Certainly I was under a lot of pressure from my family to do the latter. But my overriding instinct was to fight for my husband and to fight against the injustice. I saw heroes and brave people around me and was proud of how many Bahrainis decided that our silence would be our grave and that, at whatever cost, we could not lose the battle for freedom, dignity, and social justice.

Little things touched me. I saw how released prisoners were greeted as heroes. Busloads of people from across the country came to visit Aayat Alqurmuzi, the student who was jailed for reading a poem at the roundabout. I gained strength from my husband, who told me he made sure to laugh and make his inmates laugh in their prison cell every morning so the guards could hear and understand that despite their torture, they could not take his right to smile. In the military courts, a mother of a prisoner went home to write on the cake she prepared, "Congratulations, fifteen years." This was after she shouted at the judge that he may as well have sentenced her child to life while he was at it.

For me, these anecdotes showed that guns and tanks cannot break the spirit. And this time around, in the era of the Arab Spring, the social upheaval and the consciousness of emancipation is not one that can be repressed. Bahrainis, as Arabs, have proven this.

THE FORGOTTEN REVOLUTION

The uprising in Bahrain has been described by Al Jazeera as "the revolution that was abandoned by the Arabs, forsaken by the West, and forgotten by the world."[29] It is indeed a tragedy that the counterrevolution is perceived to have won and that this is the narrative the media has used, but I contend that the opposite is true. The counterrevolution, led by Saudi Arabia, tried to use force, violence, and direct repression to quell the uprising. However, crushing the revolution also means crushing the spirit of revolution, and this is something that neither tanks nor guns can do. Though it became physically impossible to mobilize mass gatherings and protests for a while, the uprising turned into numerous low-intensity smaller protests in many villages on a daily basis. This is still a direct challenge to the system. In addition, other creative forms of protests have emerged, such as traffic go-slows, coordinated attempts to return to the Pearl Roundabout area, and nightly chanting from rooftops. Unlikely revolutionaries have also emerged. The doctors who were sentenced to up to fifteen years for treating the injured have become figureheads in the uprising, and their discourse is one about justice, freedom, and accountability for those who tortured them.

Today, the blinding sun of torture and injustice has reached its zenith and scorched the entire island. My personal horror, and that of thousands of others, has lasted for several months and is still ongoing. My husband has experienced multiple violations that have left an everlasting physical and psychological effect on him. The trauma and wounds will not be healed through financial compensation or the reinstatement of sacked workers to their jobs. The best of the best in Bahraini society don't want material reparation, but justice will be in the form of accountability and tangible attainment of full political, economic, and human rights.

In the spirit of the Arab Spring, the revolutions of dignity, people are no longer interested in picking up crumbs of compassion thrown from the table of someone who considers himself their master. The people want the full menu of rights. Unfortunately, in Bahrain, our blood and tears are worth less than oil and interests.

THE BAHRAIN INDEPENDENT COMMISSION OF INQUIRY: TRUTH WITHOUT JUSTICE

The report the BICI published late in 2011 has caused an international stir. It confirms that mistreatment of prisoners has been systematic, and in fact "systemic," as we had said all along. At the same time, some say the report has given the regime legitimacy: since they commissioned it, they can claim that they are open to reform. But as I have said and written, it will be used as a political shield and to delay and distract real reform.

Given the pain and suffering that Bahrainis have endured firsthand, we don't need a panel of outsiders to validate this for us. I don't need anyone to tell me what happened to my husband: the scars on his back say it all. The commission's utility will be measured by its results and whether we receive justice. At the very least, I expected it to demand the immediate release of political prisoners. It will have to establish accountability—there needs to be justice for the murder, torture, and false imprisonments that have taken place. This accountability needs to go straight to the highest levels of authority in Bahrain. Finally, it should have recommended political reconciliation. Bahrain needs an explicit framework for transitioning to democracy and writing a new constitution.

A HUMAN RIGHTS CHARADE

On November 23, 2011, in one of Bahrain's royal palaces, a lavish ceremony commenced with all the pomp and ceremony of a great occasion. In the era of the so-called Arab Spring, one would expect such a celebration to herald the handover of power. But in fact it was a ceremony for the handover of the report of the BICI, a government-appointed commission with the nominal mandate of investigating the government's crimes—hardly a thing to celebrate. It must have been awkward. Most of the perpetrators of torture and abuse were sitting right there as the state's crimes were read out.

In Jaw Prison on the other side of the island, my husband Ghazi Farhan, a prisoner there for eight months, tells me that prisoners scrambled to find the analogue channel of Bahrain TV to listen to the speech of the BICI chair, Professor Mahmoud Cherif Bassiouni, after guards had switched off the satellite system that day to stop prisoners from seeing. The prisoners managed to watch half the speech before the guards discovered them and turned off the TV. A fight almost broke out between prisoners and guards.

My husband called me that evening and asked, "Did Bassiouni ask for us to be freed?" With a heavy and extremely disappointed heart, I told him, "No."

"What kind of justice is this?" he said. I did not have a reply. The commissioners let us down.

Not too far away that morning, the body of Abdulnabi Kadhem lay on the doorstep of a house in the village of Aa'li, next to his car, rammed in the side by one of the security jeeps that storm into villages on a daily basis. He was officially the forty-eighth person killed since February 14.

No one expected the King, commissioners, or any of the attendees to pay a minute's silence or even a tribute to the dead that were mentioned in the report. To the government, they were unwanted criminals and traitors. To the commissioners, they were statistics. To the majority of the Bahrainis who are fighting for change, they are martyrs who paid with their sacred blood the price of freedom.

Western journalists hailed the report as a gesture of reconciliation and a new era for Bahrain. For human rights NGOs, the report confirmed what they had been saying all along, that it was time the government of Bahrain acted.

For government loyalists, the report was like a bucket of cold water. It effectively told them they had been lied to. The government's narrative was largely debunked: there was no Iranian involvement, demonstrations were peaceful, demands of the opposition were legitimate, the opposition did not call for an Islamic republic, military tribunals were wrong, and yes, there was not just torture but systemic torture. Despite these acknowledgments, the report adopted much of the government narrative in some parts, particularly those concerning the Salmaniya hospital and the University of Bahrain—two of the most contentious events. Ultimately, despite the confirmation of the severity of abuse, the commissioners hardly made any brash recommendations, considering they avoided demanding the release of political prisoners at the very least. I believe this was a failure in their moral and professional duty. I have expressed this to them directly.

The verdict on the street was more belligerent. The February 14 Youth Coalition, the new youth movement that is driving the uprising, said the report was "honey laced with venom." The days immediately following the report saw huge mourning processions turn into massive political protests that were quelled much the same way as before.

The commissioners, who had the power to demand the release of prisoners, to incriminate those directly responsible, and to suggest tangible steps for reconciliation, failed on all three counts.

Five hundred political prisoners of the nearly three thousand arrested remain in Bahraini jails today. They must be released. My husband puts it aptly when he says, "I am in handcuffs, and my torturers get promoted." This is what Bassiouni wanted to allow the government to do.

THE DARKNESS BEFORE DAWN

I am hopeful for the future of our country. History is always on the side of the people, and we are not asking for more than what other people have achieved elsewhere. So the question isn't *if*, it's *when*.

Sometimes this uncertainty is a challenge. My husband is in jail, which is not something that I can normalize, and our fate depends on the political whim of the king. I always hope that there is no "next prison visit," that each visit will be the last. I see the old mothers hugging their handsome young sons, with a sparkle of joy in their eyes that are otherwise flooded with tears of pain. It is their tears that I would like to wipe away before my own. My husband echoes that spirit. He says that even if he were released tomorrow, he would not be able to leave in prison his newfound brothers, young and old, whose wounds he helped nurse and whose spirits he helped lift. His imprisonment has been an extraordinary experience that has changed both of us, but it has also reinforced our love and determination for each other and for our cause.

An emissary offered to make a special request for a "royal pardon" to free my husband. I told them that if they thought I would ever ask for that, despite my anguish, they have missed the entire reason for our uprising. This uprising will bring an end to this servitude. I'd rather that my husband stays in jail then emerge as a slave.

SPAIN

OVERVIEW

There is a small group of European countries hit hard by the financial crisis of 2007 and the recession that ensued where the harsh numbers tell a tale of economic catastrophe all by themselves. Spain is one. First, there is Spain's unemployment rate, stuck above 20 percent since May 2010 and rising almost continuously since the summer of 2007. For youth, it is far worse, with a rate above 40 percent. Even as jobs are scarce, the cost of living remains high. The prices of land and houses have dropped dramatically since the 2007 peak of the stupendous Spanish real estate boom—30 percent and 22 percent respectively—which has been enough to cause major problems for Spanish banks but not enough to make life affordable for most beleaguered Spaniards. The country's public debt is 60 percent the size of its gross domestic product (GDP); more to the point, at press time the rate at which Spain could borrow from the markets was at the highest level it had been since it joined the euro, pushing 7 percent for ten-year bonds. This meant it was hard for the country to independently finance the kind of economic stimulus package it desperately needed in the aftermath of the crisis. Rather, the country has turned to austerity to try to stanch the spiraling cost of debt. Not only has austerity not worked, but the measures have, predictably, made life harder on Spaniards—and likely have delayed the recovery. And, not surprisingly, as the economy has slowed, tax revenues have been disappointing, and the improvement in the deficit has been less than hoped. There has not been the lowering of interest rates that would have provided more fiscal space for the government. In fact, things have moved the other way. Today, things are bleaker than when the government started its austerity program more than two years ago. But as the failure of their policies became evident, the politicians responded by doubling down on their bets in the belief that more austerity would be the answer.

It's easy to see why bitterness and dissatisfaction have become commonplace in Spain. And yet the economic woes are only part of the story. There is also a sense that, since the first bright days of new democracy in the years after Franco, there has been a gradual loss of faith in the Spanish political system.

Enter the *indignados*. Beginning on May 15, 2011 (the reason why the group also calls itself 15M) tens of thousands of Spaniards took to the streets. The belief that direct action was required to achieve the kind of just society they wanted grew spontaneously and hit a respondent chord across a wide swath of Spanish society. Common demands—as with the Occupy Wall Street protests in the United States, the *indignados* represent a diverse range of views—included more accountable politicians, a more representative system, a reverse of the rollback of better social safety nets, and less powerful bankers. Popular movements sprouted to address particular social issues that the government was neglecting. Through it all—as the essays in this section reveal—there was an emerging passion for community involvement, even as the interest in actual voting or belief in the political system has ebbed.

On the global stage, 15M was a remarkable instance of a mass social movement in a rich country inspired by events in the developing world. Spanish protesters often cited the revolutions in Tunisia and Egypt as catalysts for their action. Directly or not, then, the *indignados* provided a crucial bridge between the revolutions of the Middle East and the uprisings of the West.

FROM NEW YORK TO MADRID AND BACK AGAIN

José Bellver

*José Bellver is a graduate student in international economy and develop-
ment as well as an activist in various social movements. He began his
work as an activist when he was an undergraduate member of a student
association. Today his involvement in social movements centers on topics
related to the environment, social justice, and heterodox and solidarity
economics. He is an active member of the 15M movement.*

On the morning of May 15th 2011, the date from which the
15M movement takes its name, I had just returned from a
short stay as a doctoral student in the United States. Even though
I wasn't in Spain in the days leading up to the protest, messages on
various social media sites made me more than aware that there was
a protest planned for that afternoon. While overseas, I had also
been carefully following what the Youth Without Future movement—a student platform that organized a successful protest in
April under the banner "Without a house, without work, without
a pension, without fear" and became one of the precedents of the
15M movement. In spite of being jetlagged from my trip, I went
to the protest with some friends. As soon as we got there, we were
energized.

A lot of people were expected to attend the 15M, but I don't think anyone—not even the organizers themselves—ever imagined the size and scale of the demonstration, or how it would ultimately develop and spread across towns and borders. What most of us agreed on was that the manifesto of the Real Democracy Now platform—the organizers of the 15M protest—was right on. The underlying message was summed up in the principal slogan of the protest: "We're not commodities in the hands of politicians and bankers."

Let's put this into context. In Spain, the bursting of the real estate bubble, the lack of judiciary independence, and the influence that big corporations have had on key government policies have generated a profound rejection of the political class by the general population, which sees rampant corruption at all levels of finance and politics. Hence the nonpartisan character of this movement, perfectly captured in two of the most often heard slogans: "They call it democracy, and it isn't" and "They don't represent us." One of the areas in which people are demanding the largest change is in the political system, which has allowed two big parties to govern the country since the return of democracy in 1977. Other proposals have emerged demanding more transparency in the financial accounts of both the parties and the politicians. There has also been a call for voting reforms allowing for more direct election of candidates by the public.

But the biggest incentive for protest derives from the economic crisis and the ensuing budget cuts, which have brought about drastic reductions in social programs and services. These so-called solutions are nothing more than a continuation of the same policies that caused the economic disaster in the first place. There is evidence—not only in Spain but throughout Europe—that shows how these policies are causing a broader recession, and possibly depression, beyond the day-to-day suffering caused by elevated rates of unemployment and precarious work situations. As young people, we are particularly affected. Even though we're probably the best educated and most qualified generation in Spain, we are no longer able to trust that we will enjoy a better life than our parents did—a consequence of the decadence of the capitalist economic system.

As a result, the 15M movement became an umbrella for multiple social battles related to economic, social justice, and environmental issues, although the defense of democracy was at the center of our demands. Therefore, the protest was made up of a diverse group of people of all ages and backgrounds, and this diversity has continued over the days, weeks, and months of the movement. A friend from my student activist days put it best: "I've run into a lot of friends and people I know who never come to these things." The breadth of this movement was what surprised me most, a clear sign that this protest was different.

The next day, May 16, I heard that some people had decided to camp out in the Puerta del Sol to continue the protest. But they were violently dislodged by the police in the middle of the second night, and there were some arrests. By midday Tuesday I received various messages calling for a protest in the same place at 8 P.M. I decided to go once again, as did many of my friends. When we arrived, there were people in the plaza, but it wasn't full, and there was concern that the police might lash out again. Some people recommended gathering into groups of a certain size so it wouldn't be considered a protest. Others gave suggestions on how to deal with a possible police response, dispensing advice like, "Stay close to someone you know," or "Grab onto each others' arms in a show of peaceful resistance." It wasn't necessary. Soon the Puerta del Sol was full to overflowing—just like New Year's Eve—and everyone was shouting slogans in unison—"The people together will never be defeated" and "These are our weapons"—while the gesture remained the same: raised arms and open palms to signal the peaceful character of the movement.

That night saw the first massive assembly—the picture of an overwhelmingly horizontal and inclusive movement. In my entire life I had never seen an assembly with so many people. Personally, I found it to be rather chaotic but not distressing. I literally got the chills when the crowd went silent to hear what was being said over the loudspeaker. This feeling of excitement is surely what gave us the patience necessary to deal with what would most likely be a long road ahead.

In this first assembly, however, the decision to stay on in the Puerta del Sol and establish a base camp was a very easy one to make, as we were all in agreement. This time, there would be many more of us camping out, in what was a clear indication of both the pulse of the movement and the challenge to the government. People began to install tents with cords that were hung from lamp-posts, building structures with canvas that people brought and pieces of cardboard found in the side streets. The crowd shouted with joy each time a sign from the original protest was hung from the front of the buildings facing the square.

As time went on, there were various kitchens and first aid stations, bathrooms, solar panels, information booths, and media relations booths. There were spaces for artistic creation, a library filled with sofas and armchairs found on the streets, and even a place for children. Some friends made a little garden next to the fountain of the Puerta del Sol. We created a small town built by the people, for the people, and there it stayed for a month. And the best part of all of this was that it wasn't only happening in Madrid. These spontaneous campgrounds were also springing up in other major cities, such as Barcelona and Seville.

The movement gained a boost from the solidarity of many people who supported it without necessarily participating in it. People brought food, blankets, and other necessities as the number of protesters multiplied. People who lived in the neighborhood pitched in, as did people who went there to work. Even bars, restaurants, and neighborhood associations helped out. Their support bolstered our confidence, just as the police attempts to suppress our movement made us all the more determined.

Later that week I decided to become a more active participant in the movement, and so I went to the tent occupied by the Internal Coordination Commission. They suggested that I join one of the thematic work groups that were just getting started, to discuss more specific topics and proposals. Initially there were five groups, one each dealing with politics, the economy, social issues, the environment, and education and culture. I joined the group dealing with economic issues, although I also went to a few of the assemblies organized by the environment group. Together with another guy, I helped take the minutes for the first assembly of the economy group. It took some time to finish a final draft, not only because we wanted the proposals that we had agreed upon to be as clear as possible but also because there was an argument among the group of people gathered in the booth where we were working. One girl was scandalized by how many proposals the economy group had produced and viewed most of what we were recommending as outright radical. She thought we were overreaching. But her attitude completely contradicted one of the central phrases of the camp manifest: "We want it all; we want it now." We decided that one or two people were not going to censor or rewrite what many more people had already decided in the assembly. But this conflict clearly demonstrated that two sides can coexist in a movement under the same sense of indignation. Our general feeling was the same, but our approach was different.

In fact, many of the proposals that came out of these assemblies were the result of years of analysis by many earlier social movements. But our predecessors had never managed to do what this movement was accomplishing—bringing people into the streets and plazas of their towns to talk and debate about the different ways of managing our lives. We were relating to each other on a level like never before. The enormous numbers of people who attended these assemblies showed just how hungry people were to share opinions, even if they didn't know each other and came from very different walks of life. They all shared the frustration of seeing how their quality of life was increasingly diminishing while the political and economic powers stood by.

Not only did I attend the largest assembly, I was also present for the longest assembly, which lasted nearly an entire day. This was a coordination assembly among working groups that came about because there was concern that the movement was falling prey to the media's demand that it quickly come up with a list of specific proposals. A number of proposals from the policy group had already gotten out, and the majority of those of us who were present thought that we should at least add a few economic proposals to the list under the caveat that they were minimum requirements. But some assembly members insisted on blocking any proposal deemed to have been done in haste, regardless of its well-considered content. The only way out of this conflict was for each working group to make its own decisions on what proposals to release, and when.

This story helps illustrate the confusion that can sometimes occur between consensus and unanimity. Fortunately, the creation of an organizing commission in the assemblies has started to resolve this problem, gradually smoothing out our methods of collective decision making. This organizing commission is crucial for the movement. However, although searching for consensus can delay decisions, it also brings about true democracy and fosters more active citizenship, which is critical not only for achieving the desired changes but also for making sure these changes are lasting.

After nearly a month of discussions, workshops, and exchanges of documents and information, the economic assembly reached a consensus on about twenty proposals from the various work groups in the areas of employment, business, housing, economic policy, financial systems, and global economic relations. These proposals ranged from the cancellation of aid to the banks to more progressive taxation (with the wealthy bearing the greater burden). There were also proposals for the defense of quality public services, the rejection of privatization, the sharing or reduction of work hours, the stabilization of the value of wages and pensions, the elimination of tax havens, and a tax levy on speculative transactions.

Today, the economy group and the other groups keep working on multiple initiatives ranging from dissemination of information to training, discussion, and implementation of concrete actions. At the same time, many working groups have been established in neighborhoods and towns. And so, from its grassroots beginning, the movement continues to cultivate success not only across the rest of Spain but also around the world. I'm proud and gratified to see how some of the friends I made during my stay in the United States, and with whom I talked about the 15M movement in its early days, got involved in their own protests across the ocean and right in the eye of the hurricane: Wall Street.

WE ARE THE 99%

Sara López Martín and Javier García Raboso

Sara López Martín is thirty-two years old and has a PhD in political science. She works on issues of human rights and torture prevention. She has participated in the anti-globalization movement, and more recently in the squatter and alternative media movements.

Javier García Raboso is twenty-nine years old. He has a degree in sociology and is an expert in mediation and topics of social integration. Javier has worked with young people and populations at risk of social exclusion. He is also an active participant in groups that support the plight of the Saharawi people.

Sara and Javier met in the 15M movement and have experienced the process together from the very beginning. They were in the Puerta del Sol campground from the start, and they both participated in the Legal Commission.

It was an incredible and heartening scene to behold. We were many, thousands in fact. It seemed as if the feeling of indignation was beginning to take root, grow, and spread. More and more, ordinary Spanish citizens were becoming convinced that we needed to raise our voices once and for all against this crazy system that made us bear the consequences of the excesses of others.

"We're not commodities in the hands of politicians and bankers," the signs proclaimed. Voting every four years wasn't enough anymore. It was no more than crumbs of a democracy that had shown itself to be highly insufficient at channeling our demands, which didn't find an echo in any parliament or media outlet of the system. "No, no, no, they don't represent us!" we chanted energetically. It's possible that we didn't have a concrete idea of what we wanted, but we knew perfectly well what we didn't want: to pay the consequences of a crisis that we didn't cause. Nor did we want our political class to betray us by rescuing the powerful executioners at the expense of most of society and inflicting pain upon the weakest. So there was a common desire that united us. We were fed up, *indignado*, and we wanted our voices to be heard throughout the streets. Even if they pretended not to hear us in parliament, this historic theft would not go unnoticed.

We, along with many others, arrived at the May 15 protest called by Real Democracy Now. We had been involved in previous protests against the crisis, convinced that there was a systemic problem within unchecked capitalism that generated poverty and environmental destruction around the planet. We had seen young people becoming active in protests in other parts of Europe and thought that now it was our turn. But we also expected this protest to be like all the others—people take to the streets, they go home, and everything stays the same. This was not the case.

The protest was festive and peaceful; we were simply making ourselves heard. In this atmosphere, the last thing we expected was the brutal force that the police used against us. We didn't deserve such treatment. They wanted to make us pay for daring to dissent and express ourselves. It was clear that they wanted to spread fear so that this kind of protest wouldn't be repeated. That's a curious way to practice democracy. During the protests, numerous people were hurt or detained. Because of this glaring injustice, calm did not prevail. Slowly, those of us who had been scattered, fleeing from the blows, the truncheons, and the handcuffs, began gathering again in the Puerta del Sol, but not everyone was there. The air was filled with an atmosphere of stupor, indignation, and anger. Not only were we suffering the effects of a crisis that we did not cause, we were paying the price by daring to complain about it.

The politicians wanted to silence us with blows and jail. They didn't have the right to do this to us. Each person who was hurt or detained was part of all of us. We were them, and they were us. The repression struck us all. So, sick of always getting the same treatment, we stayed on in the square to protest. This time, we had had enough. We had hit bottom. Hours passed, and a few dozen of our more daring and determined colleagues even decided to stay overnight. We were among them.

By the next afternoon, more people arrived to join us. We called an assembly, and now we were numbering in the hundreds. No one was willing to let the beatings and arrests happen again. We formed a large circle, each person holding onto the next so that we could resist eviction but do so peacefully. During this response to the police brutality, the infrastructure commissions, those of direct and legal action, came into being. The two of us decided to be part of the legal commission even though we weren't lawyers. Like everyone there at the time, we brought whatever we knew to the table—our experience in mediation and the knowledge that we had acquired as members of other social movements.

There was a crackle of energy in the air that second night; we were all excited to get to work. But by the wee hours, most of us were asleep when all of a sudden we were awakened by the sound of a police car screeching to a halt. The officer got out of the car, strode toward us, and issued an ultimatum: we could either leave by our own will or leave by force. There were dozens of policemen against a hundred of us. The tension rose quickly as we moved toward the center of the plaza, forming a wall of resistance with our arms to protect and support each other. The policemen moved into formation, and there we were, face to face. We tried to diffuse the tension by explaining the situation to them, but there was little we could do. They had already decided that they were going to remove us from the plaza by any means necessary.

These were frightening circumstances, but we talked amongst ourselves and agreed out loud and unanimously that we would not move willingly from that plaza. The police responded as they had been ordered, and one by one, they broke through our human shield and soon dispersed us with a relentless series of punches, pushes, and threats. Our belongings were scattered, people were hurt, and one person was arrested. We ended up split into two groups, one on each side of the plaza, and we began to raise our hands in a peaceful sign of resistance against this eviction. But the police response was the same. While threatening to hit us, they pushed us toward the nearby Gran Via, where they surrounded us and made us show our identification cards before they dissolved the group.

Later that morning, on May 17, dozens of stubborn colleagues then got together in a social center. Energized by their thirst for justice, they decided to call a new protest for that same afternoon in the same place where everything had begun, in response to the new wave of repression that we had suffered. Messages went flying over the Internet. We used Facebook, Twitter, and other social networks to organize a protest without precedent. That afternoon, the plaza was full of *indignados*, and once again we were thousands, tens of thousands. The amazing show of solidarity and support caught all of us by surprise. It filled us with hope and made us realize that we weren't alone in this, that our problems were those of the large majority of people. And for the politicians, media outlets, and security forces, this gathering was like a glass of cold water, a lesson in humility. They got a bitter surprise that they could no longer treat the voice of the people in this terrible way, by ignoring some and repressing others.

Over the next two days, our numbers continued to swell into the thousands. Soon tents were erected all over the square, and groups of us were organizing logistical commissions to handle feeding the crowds, addressing health concerns, and decorating the site with protest signs. More than eighty lawyers and advisors formed a legal commission to organize the proposed protests. Before we knew it, the square became a parallel city with all of the ad hoc infrastructure necessary to distribute information and identify and resolve needs on the fly. In short, we'd established an activist's utopia.

The disconnect between this massive reality and the discourse of those who were pointing accusing fingers was spectacular. While thousands of people were constantly coming by to encourage us, sign petitions, and generally show their support, the media and the political class initially had a very different attitude. It took the press a few days to realize what it had on its hands. First, the *Washington Post* had to do a front-page story on 15M. Until then, the Spanish media would merely collect small, decontextualized anecdotes, such as, "My name is Javi, I'm twenty-eight and unemployed." Foreign journalists had to cover 15M as a story before our own media would recognize what we were doing as an authentic social revolt.

The political class also changed its tune. While right-wing extremists began by describing us as "dirty," "flea-ridden," and "lazy," the majority began to show some half-hearted commitment. With few exceptions, no one dared to openly attack us, but neither did they take us seriously and answer our questions. There was no direct police intervention in the plaza, nor would there be during the entire rest of the month, although there was always an atmosphere of tension.

The campsite lasted a week and achieved its first goal of demonstrating that it was possible to assemble with horizontal and efficient management, and to open spaces for independent political dialogue without intermediaries. We also achieved massive support for the call for disobedience against the ban on public protest the day before the municipal elections on May 22. One of the protest signs read: "Politicians, beware: the public declares the electoral commission illegal." This idea of legitimacy versus legality was a central hallmark of our bid for political regeneration from below.

The elections came and went, and there we stayed. Nothing had changed. ("Our dreams don't fit into voting urns," read many signs.) The campsite was restructured. Spaces were redistributed, streets were planned, and new commissions were created. In no time at all there was a library and a nursery, a cleaning service, and even physiotherapists and psychologists who set up shop in small tents. But it wasn't just services that were extended. We realized we needed to move beyond mere protest and come up with solutions, so we formed work groups on everything from the environment to education in order to form consensus on the political lines of our movement.

For three weeks, the Sol campground became a beehive of activity and extraordinary creativity. It was amazing to walk around the surrounding streets and find assemblies in every plaza and on each street corner. Where did all these people with a need to express themselves come from? And where were they before the protests? The real question was not what we were doing before but what we were going to do now. The greatest experience of autonomous management of a space that Madrid had experienced since the Civil War had inspired us and taught us a great deal, but we were left with some dilemmas. We were struggling with accumulated exhaustion from weeks of encampment and facing the dawning realization that achieving consensus in an assembly of thousands was a daunting challenge. We also wanted to spread the movement to areas outside the square while maintaining that spark of indignation that energized us in the first place.

It took us weeks to decide to pack up shop and move the activity into other towns and neighborhoods. At the time of this writing, almost six months after the first protests, more than one hundred twenty assemblies are active in the greater Madrid area. Our movement managed to insert topics into the media and political agendas that would have been unheard of before, bringing issues like corruption, property evictions, and the role of the banks in the financial crisis much more to the fore. We also succeed in forming a new generation of activists committed to developing collective responses to problems previously considered to be the burdens of the individual, such as halting evictions, for example. In short, we've taken several crucial steps toward the creation of a more humane and active civil society.

In this period of the "democratic spring," a network of associations has sprung up in a society virtually demobilized after forty years of Franco and thirty years of a weak and not particularly participatory democracy. Channels have been created that seek to direct, at the very least, the expression of discontent. Spaces have been opened for public debate in places where they simply did not exist before. These, in our opinion, are several of the major contributions of the 15M movement toward the formation of a true democratic culture in the Spanish state.

We were fighting for change, and change was possible. Or at least that was the case during the months that followed in the Puerta del Sol. The events of May 2011 showed that we, too, were capable of demanding changes in a political and economic system that doesn't satisfy the needs of its citizens. We effected change just like the Icelanders, Saharawis, Tunisians, Egyptians, and Greeks did before us, and like other Europeans and Americans did after us. And just like so many people who wait for their chance to rise up, and will do so in the future. Because we are the 99 percent.

"THINK GLOBAL, ACT LOCAL":
NEIGHBORHOOD AND TOWN ASSEMBLIES

Alejandra Machín Álvarez

Alejandra Machín Álvarez is a young economist who specializes in international and development economics. She is currently unemployed, but her dream is to work as a researcher in the area of economic development. She has always been interested in issues of social inequality and has been involved in politics since her time at the university. Alejandra has been active in the 15M movement from the start, but her involvement deepened considerably with the establishment of the neighborhood assemblies. She is currently a member of the communication commission of the Popular Assembly of the Salamanca District in Madrid.

"Think global, act local." That was the first phrase that came to mind when I heard that the 15M movement—the name given to the 2011 protest movement in Spain that grew out of the May 15th demonstration in Madrid—was leaving the Puerta de Sol, the central square of our capital, to set up shop in neighborhoods across Spain.

I always liked that expression. Hidden in its meaning seemed to be the solution to many of the social, economic, or environmental problems that surrounded me. But as a specialist in economic development and international economics, I was always more focused on the global aspect of things. And yet, on May 28, 2011, this phrase took on a special significance for the 15M movement—and for Spanish politics in general—because that was the day the Commission of Neighborhoods of Sol agreed to establish the first popular assemblies of neighborhoods and towns of Madrid. These General Assemblies are forums for much broader political participation by ordinary citizens, allowing them to weigh in on a variety of issues that might otherwise be decided upon unilaterally by the government authorities in power.

The assemblies have two specific goals: the first is to make the government aware of injustice related to the economic crisis. The assemblies do not attempt to replace local or state government. Instead, they aim to assert social rights on specific topics, such as the need to fight for direct democracy and against the excess protection given to banks at the expense of citizens or cuts in public services. The second is to come up with alternative solutions to the problems that beset us all. For example, the Assembly of the Unemployed in Madrid and Barcelona has created a cooperative to help unemployed people become self-employed. The assemblies also try to prevent evictions and have created mutual support networks to help out in neighborhoods.

All of the assemblies' actions and debates are open to participation by all citizens. Those individuals or groups that are not represented in the assemblies do not have to abide by assembly decisions if they disagree with them. However, in cases where there are two competing interests, the assembly tries to negotiate a consensus between the two parties.

A few hundred assemblies came about as a result of the May 28 agreement to establish these forums, and more than one hundred twenty are still functioning in Madrid.

For me, the idea of forming neighborhood and town assemblies is in itself revolutionary. This is because moving to a truly horizontal and inclusive political process, built from the ground up, represents a critical transformation in a country's political system.

The localization movement is a new way of relating with our fellow citizens that does away with the individualism and isolation in which we have lived. My neighbors had always been people I saw in the doorway or the elevator, people with whom I shared a building only. There was never a feeling of neighborhood life. And now, suddenly, in trying to build a direct and horizontal structure of political participation, I had to start talking and working with a bunch of strangers called "neighbors." Imagine that!

This process was happening almost simultaneously in the majority of Spanish cities. It is not an isolated movement that is limited to Madrid and its environs but instead a paradigm change I have seen for myself when I've visited assemblies in Almeria, Tenerife, and elsewhere in the world.

On May 28, I attended my first neighborhood assembly, the Popular Assembly of the Salamanca District. I was one of the first people to arrive. I had made plans to meet a friend, and we sat together on the ground, waiting to see what would happen, feeling both excited and skeptical. Little by little, more neighbors arrived, until finally, we were surrounded by a crowd of about three hundred fifty people.

HOW IT WORKS: ORGANIZATION AND COORDINATION

Our first assembly was mostly about logistics. We agreed on the meeting place, the schedule, the first commissions, and most importantly, the model for making decisions. We were going to decide through unanimous consensus, which would ensure that we were creating something for everyone involved, empowering us, and allowing us to make it our own. But it brings problems. Assemblies become long and onerous when two or more ideas conflict and there is no way to make them work together.

Here's where the organizing committee comes into play. It is necessary to have a group of people charged with making the debates flow and keeping things respectful, a commission that evaluates the mood and the strengths of the people assembled to facilitate debate and the work at hand.

Another crucial feature in the structure of the assembly is access to information, because without true and ample information, you can't have critical and constructive thought. The Communication Commission is in charge of making available the necessary information to function and to coordinate each commission with the others. Normally, in the neighborhood and town assemblies, there are also thematic commissions or work groups whose job is to work on the battle fronts that are of particular importance to the public, such as the Political Commission, the Economic Commission, the Public Services (Health and Education) Commission, and the Housing Commission. All of these commissions get together weekly to develop proposals that they then take to their neighborhood assembly for consensus. All decisions or interventions must be approved by the assembly before they can be considered legitimate.

The activity of these assemblies is not limited to discussion and theorizing about the principal problems of the Spanish society, which is why direct action is a key component of these forums. All demands or problems must be addressed by a concrete action that helps to resolve them, whether they be protests or efforts to stop evictions, or even street performances. Just as important as what needs to be done is the manner in which it is done, and how people are involved. This is where the infrastructure and diffusion committees come into play.

The summer months were especially fruitful in terms of these kinds of direct actions, and many of the assemblies forged their first alliances. The neighborhood and town assemblies called their first state demonstration for June 19, a day to remember.[30] All of the neighborhood and town assemblies of Madrid organized into columns that marched through the streets of the capital to meet in the Plaza de Neptuno, at the door of the Congress of Deputies, to protest together against the Euro Pact. The same kind of thing happened in many Spanish cities.

This protest was followed by many others, such as the arrival into Madrid of the *marchas indignadas* on July 23.[31] This demonstration was made up of people who had come by foot from different parts of Spain. There was a whole protocol surrounding how these people would be accompanied on the road and how they would be received in Madrid, and this would not have been possible without coordination among different assemblies across Spain.

The effectiveness of these assemblies in communicating and executing the wishes of the people continues to improve. Through the Neighborhood and Town Assembly of Madrid (APM), groups from different neighborhoods and surrounding towns get together every fifteen days to transmit collective decisions. APM's Web page is fundamental for this level of coordination (http://madrid .tomalaplaza.net/) because it allows us to communicate amongst ourselves so we can carry out actions and debates together. It has been an essential too.

WORK IN THE ASSEMBLIES

Ever since the end of May, assemblies in all the cities, neighborhoods, and towns of Spain have been hard at work. Many of us have the feeling of being immersed in a very exciting project that will ultimately change the reality in which we live. But, for now, our involvement demands enormous dedication and energy. In order to effect real change, you need conviction and time—lots of time. The level of commitment required is so intense that sometimes it takes you away from your regular social and family life.

It can be tiring and frustrating. There are times when you get home after a hard day at work in the assemblies or meetings and, for those who are lucky, from a paying job, and you're really upset. You spent days putting all your effort into a proposal that does not turn out how you had hoped, leaving a bad taste in your mouth. But this is par for the course since ultimately our culture and our way of life has accustomed us to thinking that we have the right to have all that we want when we want it, without having to wait or to work or to take into account the opinions of others. The maxims of "here and now" and "if you want something to turn out well, you'd better do it yourself," are embedded in our minds. But these are false notions. Things turn out better when you count on the creativity and effort of many people to make them happen. Immediacy is not a synonym for a job well done. "We go slowly, but we go far," is another one of 15M's great slogans. You have to summon patience to work by assembly, but this patience bears great fruit.

These small autonomous assemblies have thrown up thousands of initiatives, but not all of them have worked. We face so many problems at present, and there is such a great need to find solutions for all of them. It is amazing to see what the neighborhood or town assemblies can do by making people aware of the injustices of forced evictions or by serving as aids or mediators for neighbors with a problem in their town hall or neighborhood association. At the same time, these assemblies greatly augment the level of democratic participation that has been sadly lacking in our country. They have forever changed the way in which we relate to each other and carry out politics.

The work of the assemblies is complemented by that of the thematic platforms and work groups on which we rely when we want to work on a specific topic. Among the most important of these groups is the platform for those affected by mortgages (PAH) in the fight against evictions, the platform against the privatization of public services, the Canal de Isabel II platform (which is fighting against the privatization of the water system in Madrid), and the work groups of Sol, which include such topics as the economy, politics, the general elections of November 20, education, and health.

These assemblies have also had a critical impact on the social awareness and lifestyle of their participants. They are spaces where cooperation is valued above competition and the belief that "he who has the most is worth the most" no longer reigns. More than voting, the only way we have to decisively influence a change in our prevailing economic and social system is through lifestyle choices and, in particular, how we consume. One of the most relevant topics that we talk about in our assembly, and one that has special significance for me, is that of responsible consumption and the creation of mutual support networks. Thanks to these networks, I now have shared Internet with my neighbors, and I have been able to get rid of my old boom box, giving it to someone else who needs it more than I do.

The assemblies have also become a valuable educational and cultural forum for neighborhoods.[32] Workshops have been held on everything from ethical banking to active listening and political participation. Other assembly activities, such as concerts, group painting, theater, and poetry recitals, combine fun with political protest, with the intention of encouraging neighborhood life and bringing culture to the streets.

City, town, and neighborhood assemblies have been extremely active in their nearly six months of life. They continue to show a different way of carrying out politics, one that is horizontal and inclusive and without precedent in Spanish history. The movement may have begun in Madrid, but the assemblies are sprouting up across Spain, and it is not fair to give one city the ownership of an entire movement. What would Puerta del Sol be without the rays of sunshine that come from across all corners of the land?

The struggle continues in your neighborhood, in your square![33]

A SOCIAL AWAKENING: HISTORY
OF THE PROTESTS AGAINST EVICTIONS

Jonay Martín Valenzuela

Jonay Martín Valenzuela is a participant in the 15M movement. He has been active in the protests against evictions in the greater Madrid area and works in the communications and diffusion commission of the Popular Assembly of the Salamanca District in Madrid. He also collaborates with the platform for those affected by mortgages (PAH), as well as the platform dedicated to helping the activists detained in the protest for decent housing. On a state level, Jonay is involved in the movement assemblies. While he has been involved in activism to some degree in the past, he has recently dedicated himself to the movement.

Jonay completed high school and in order to become independent began working at the age of seventeen. A hardworking and ambitious youth, he has worked in a variety of roles—as a cook, waiter, and fruit and clothes seller, among others. Jonay quickly saw his new mission in May 2011, after the soap shop where he worked closed, and he lost his job and became another victim of the recession. Presently, he is studying for the university entrance exam. He plans to study for a career in social education.

In the middle of June 2011, I dragged myself out of bed at the crack of dawn to meet a friend from my neighborhood assembly. It was an unusually early start for me, which tells you how motivated I was to attend my first protest against the evictions that had been creating so much suffering for families across Spain. Still half-asleep, we fired ourselves up on the way to the Tetuán neighborhood in the north of Madrid by talking about the conditions under which the eviction was supposed to happen. For us, the legal justifications had no moral or ethical grounds.

If anything, the lack of ethics of the markets that govern the banks and economic system has played a huge role in these evictions. It was the banks and financial entities that gave these loans and mortgages *en masse* without wanting to assume the risks. Purely for profit, they force evictions and debt payments on people who no longer have a home or the money needed to pay the mortgage.

The crisis that was causing these evictions was a long time in coming. Real estate prices in Spain rose 201 percent from 1985 to 2007. This, together with the out-of-control ease in which credit was made available, meant that many Spaniards got mortgages for astronomic amounts and on terms way beyond twenty years. When the real estate bubble burst in 2008, the demand for housing stalled, and construction companies and real estate developers stopped building and selling houses. Since the real estate sector is one of the principal engines of the Spanish economy, this halt in activity had catastrophic consequences on state revenues and particularly employment. In 2008, many families found themselves with at least one person unemployed in the household and burdened with paying off a mortgage at a growing rate of interest, forcing them into default. The banks reacted with foreclosures and evictions.

Discussing these conditions did more to wake us up and get our pulses racing than three double espressos. So by the time we made it to the outskirts of Tetuán, we were completely alert. But we had no idea what to expect. When we got to the street where the gathering was happening, we saw about three hundred people who had the same face of uncertainty that we did. We were spread out all over the street, with more people in the doorway and maybe fifty people already inside. In effect, we had formed a human barrier against the dictates of the markets.

As the morning went on, the news outlets arrived. The police watched impassively while passersby looked on in amazement. More people joined us, and shouts of support could be heard periodically from cars and neighboring windows. The chanting was constant: "We're going to stop this eviction"; "The people united will never be defeated"; "No human being is illegal"; "No, no, they don't represent us"; "We won't pay for your crisis"; and "North to south, east to west, the fight will continue whatever it takes."

Finally, by 2 P.M., we heard that the eviction was being delayed. The person who was affected came outside to confirm this and express his gratitude. Accompanied by his lawyer, he talked to the press and shook hands with as many of as he could in a gesture of "mission accomplished." Now all that was left to do was to go to the financial institution that had given the eviction order.

We found a branch of the bank a few streets away. Seeing about forty of us arrive, the office workers got scared and locked the door. In a spirit of peace and dialogue, we asked to speak to the head of the branch. They said no. We opened up a path so that clients of the bank could easily get in and out of the bank, and this defused some of the tension inside. The clients began to leave, and we organized a sit-in, directing our chants to passersby. We explained that we were gathered there precisely because this was the branch that had begun eviction proceedings. We explained why we were there to those who chose to stop and ask, and we described the conditions under which the eviction order was processed. Each person we spoke with congratulated us for our actions. I still have the photo of the paper that we hung on the branch, which says, "This office is closed because society is waking up." We left the bank branch around 4:30 P.M.

It was a small victory, but it was just the beginning. The aim of our movement is twofold: to call attention to this widespread injustice and to help families avoid losing their homes, which in a global economic crisis with massive unemployment further limits all possibilities to get ahead. What's more, it's inhumane. People have been evicted who can't even get out of bed because they have terminal cancer. People are losing their homes because they took on a mortgage at €600 a month and now find that they are paying €1,400 a month. In a country with five million empty houses, these bankrupt families are made homeless.

It's only because of our protest efforts that a relative handful of families have been saved from this fate. Close to one hundred evictions in Spain were stopped between May and August 2011. But it's nowhere near enough. We've been told that more than forty evictions happen from Monday to Friday each week in Madrid. Given this high number, relatively few people who are being evicted are asking for help from the assemblies or platforms like the PAH. But at least now the Judicial Commission finds itself with an opposition and peaceful resistance in the doorways, in the streets, and most importantly, in both the individual and collective consciousness.

We've been growing, developing as people and as activists, and learning a lot in the school of the street, at roundtables and in the neighborhood and town assemblies. The public is getting more complete information about the causes of the evictions and the reasons why an insolvent family is forced out onto the street, and their increasing awareness is creating a groundswell of support for our movement.

Ordinary citizens' perception of our protest movement has been enhanced by the fact that our demonstrations have been peaceful and well-organized, with the primary aim of protecting the families facing eviction. We also focus on disseminating information and diffusing the tensions on both sides. In every protest against the evictions, we are in direct contact with the family. Some colleagues from the PAH stay inside, giving support to the family while we communicate with them through the intercom when there is news from the outside.

In the streets, we get new information and pass it on to our colleagues. The doorway becomes a school where we can hear the opinions of those who are gathered inside and outside the property, and learn from their experiences.

Of course, not all of these eviction demonstrations go smoothly, and some situations can be downright explosive. The story of the eviction in Pueblo Nuevo, a neighborhood in the east of Madrid, is very different from the first eviction protest I witnessed in Tetuán. We had to go to the same place twice. The first time, riot police lined both sides of the street, and the air was fraught with tension. Still, we were able to maintain the peace. Even with all this police presence, the Judicial Commission decided to postpone this first eviction attempt.

The second attempt at eviction was much more violent than the first. We got word that the judge who was in charge of the case had given the order to process the eviction without fail. We put out a call both individually and on the assembly level and managed to get the word out effectively. We decided to meet an hour earlier than usual—the judicial order tends to arrive around 10:30 A.M., and we told people to be there at 7 A.M. We were worried that there was going to be a larger than usual police presence because of what the judge had said. Unfortunately, our extra efforts were for naught.

The first activists arrived at the doorway by 7:30, but as they waited for more people to arrive, they were beaten and scattered by the police. A few managed to get inside the doorway, and a friend, P., even managed to get inside the house. By the time I arrived at 8 A.M., the scene was bleak. I counted more than twenty police vans parked near the metro exits, cutting off the entrances to the street where the eviction protest was taking place. The police were removing our banners and emblems, and asking for identification from everyone who came out of the metro or anyone who appeared to sympathize with the cause of the protesters. They asked me for my national identify card twice and threatened people in the crowd by saying, "We have your number," and "Your names are going onto a list."

Twice, I asked the officers if they understood why we were there. I asked them whether they realized that they too were mortgaged and that, given the case, we would also go to protest the eviction of a police officer. Toning it down a little, they told us that they understood our cause and supported our fight, but they reminded us that they had to follow orders. When I asked them whether they had been told to speak to us in such a threatening tone, they didn't answer. I asked whether they knew that civil disobedience, in addition to being an obligation, is also a right. They didn't answer. I rebuked them by saying that if they shared our fight, as they had said, then how was it that we were each going in different directions. "If we keep going this way, we'll never advance," I said. Once again, they didn't respond, but they let us go on. I remember the image of their silent faces, but I'm sad to say some of my colleagues also remember the mark of their truncheons.

There was resistance until the end, but they finally evicted the woman we were trying to help. We ran through the streets, calling out to people and explaining what had happened to passersby. About a hundred of us went to the door of the local council to demand a solution for the evicted family and to fill out a formal complaint. But the reality was we'd just faced our first defeat. We also visited a branch of the bank that had given the eviction proceeding.

The circumstances are always changing, and each protest against the evictions is its own particular world. In some of the protests, the riot police continue their presence but don't act; in others they lash out powerfully and indiscriminately. In some cases the Judicial Commission doesn't appear, and in others they do. Sometimes hundreds of people attend the protest, sometimes fifty or less, as was the case of Puente Vallecas, located in the eastern neighborhood of Vallecas, where just twenty of us were able to stop the policemen who tried to get to the doorway.

What all the protests have in common is that more and more, the media is paying attention to events that they had previously ignored or dismissed as irrelevant. Before May 2011, they didn't see hundreds of people gathered in the doorways, so evictions weren't considered enough of a story. But now the news outlets can't help but notice what's going on.

Legally, our fight is advancing as well. A proposal made by the PAH to have banks cancel the debt in exchange for handing over the keys to a property is now a part of the national conversation. Such a change would put Spanish property laws more in line with the U.S. system, in which people can walk away from the mortgage by turning over their houses—unlike in Europe, where you can lose your home and still be liable for those monthly payments. The protests organized by the PAH for September 25 were also a success. The nine colleagues who had been detained for holding a sit-in in Puerta de Sol, the main square in Madrid, in the 2006 protest for decent housing received widespread support in the judicial proceedings. Five were absolved, and the other four received prison sentences, but because they don't have prior convictions, they will not serve time. So in some ways the tide is turning in our favor.

But not all is good news. Puerta de Hierro, a neighborhood in the west of Madrid, is still fighting. At the end of July 2011, the Madrid authorities decided to demolish most of the houses of more than fifty-seven families, many of whom had been living on this land since the 1960s. These families never received official permission to build on this land, but it is only now, when the property has increased significantly in value, that they are being evicted. These evictions often take place in the middle of the night, and residents are forced to abandon their homes with little warning to avoid getting caught in the demolition process. But the residents refuse to leave the land despite the harsh and unsanitary living conditions. (The mayor is obliged to remove the rubble left behind from the razed houses, but he does not.) Many 15M participants, along with others, have tried to help these families by rebuilding their homes, but their efforts have turned into a game of cat and mouse with the authorities, who go back to demolish these rebuilt dwellings once again.

In the first week of November, some colleagues were beaten in a doorway in the Madrid neighborhood of Hortaleza, and Ch., one of the leaders behind the PAH movement in Madrid, was detained. So many of us have had to pay a heavy price. But we know it is the only way to evolve our social conscience. And we have the moral obligation to walk this way. If we don't do anything, nothing will change. It's time to wake up in the name of justice, progress, and human rights, before it's too late.

The fight continues, always, no matter what it takes.

CHILE

OVERVIEW

During 2011, the Chilean political agenda was taken over by students' protests, which started in May as a demand for enhancing public education. Students were able to organize the most massive street demonstrations since the return of democracy in 1990, and week after week, thousands of Chileans from all ages and social origins marched with them, calling the right-wing government of President Sebastián Piñera to end inequality in access to education. In Santiago alone, there were forty-two marches, while public universities and high schools across the country remained occupied and paralyzed by students during most of the year.

The roots of the Chileans' indignation are in 1980, when Augusto Pinochet's dictatorship implemented a new education policy advised by a group of neoliberal economists known as "Chicago Boys"—all alumni of Chicago University—who believed that education should follow market rules. Public universities started to charge tuition and dramatically decreased their budgets, and the opening of private universities was promoted. Even though profit in higher education is forbidden in Chile, a loophole allows private universities to earn profit and at the same time not pay taxes. During the two decades that followed the dictatorship, the enrollment in higher education more than doubled, mostly in private universities of doubtful quality, while loans and scholarships were implemented but the regulatory framework remained unchanged. At the same time, primary and secondary public education improved, but Chile's public education system is still one of the most segregated and unequal in the world. As a result, Chilean universities perpetuate social inequality, with poor students having little alternative but to attend low-quality universities, and rich students attending the best ones.

The Concertación, the coalition that ruled for twenty years, lost the elections in 2010 in part because people felt that despite economic growth, they were not able to significantly reduce inequality. When Piñera took office in 2010, he appointed a "Chicago Boy" who owned a private university as minister of education. He announced a reform to higher education, the details of which were never known, but the general thrust was that it would give equal treatment to private and public universities.

The announcements fueled students' protests, who demanded the end of inequality in education, the end of profit making for universities, and an improvement in quality. They were able to engage most of the country in their fight. At the peak of the conflict, polls showed that 80 percent of citizens supported the demands of the students, while support for the government fell sharply to 27 percent. What started out as a movement to strengthen the public education system and end the illegal profit making of private universities broadened into a fundamental questioning of Chile's democratic institutions. The protest evolved into a strong demand for more equality in one of the most unequal countries in the world.

The student movement was organized by the Confederation of Chilean Students (Confech) and had two visible leaders: Camila Vallejo, a communist student from the University of Chile, and Giorgio Jackson, the president of the Federation of Students of the Catholic University of Chile (FEUC).

STUDENTS OF CHANGE:
HOW A CALL FOR EDUCATION ACCESS
BECAME A CRY FOR TRUE DEMOCRACY

Giorgio Jackson

Giorgio Jackson, twenty-four, is studying civil engineering at the Catholic University of Chile. Until November 2011, he was the spokesperson for Confech and president of the Federation of Students of the Catholic University of Chile (FEUC). He was one of the leaders of the student movement that changed the crux of political discussion in Chile through massive protests in the streets.

I was motivated to get involved in student organizations as a result of the social and community work that I did for an NGO called "A Roof for Chile," which builds housing for the homeless. But there comes a time when you realize that volunteer work doesn't break the cycle of poverty. In the FEUC, they asked me to run a training program for workers, and that's where I began to understand that education could change people's lives. I started learning more about higher education reform and began to participate in the university movement known as New Action (NAU), where I ran for office and served as territorial counselor within the engineering faculty at the Catholic University of Chile. Later, I was asked to run for president of the FEUC. When I was elected, I was happy because it felt like the NAU movement changed the course of my life. It transformed my social vocation into a political one, and this has clearly changed the direction of my future.

In 2010, we began working with other federations in Confech and realized that there was an opportunity to do something with more significance, but we never imagined to what degree. Within Confech it was well understood that it was going to be a difficult year, and the fact that there was a right-wing government in power that was almost 100 percent opposed to all of Confech's principles made us realize that we had to act in unison. This was pure pragmatism—it was David versus Goliath.

When the government announced that 2011 was going to be the year of education, those in power had no idea that we would make this literally come true. We didn't understand the government's thinking. How was it possible that they wanted to further privatize the educational system in Chile? Spending on education there is already privatized and families spend a high percentage of their income on higher education, according to the Organization for Economic Cooperation and Development (OECD).

Another element that made it possible for all this to come to a head was the fact that the generation that led a 2006 high school student movement was now in the university. Many were in debt. Others had not gone on to university or had been forced to drop out halfway. In Chile, this generation is known as the "children of democracy."

We grew up in the absence of dictatorship, without a curfew and without seeing armed forces on the street. This made us freer. All of our lives we've been able to say what we think without being afraid of repression, and that's key when it comes to forming a social movement. We don't owe anything to the political coalition that participated in the return of democracy because we were born into democracy. We didn't have to be eternally grateful, and instead we could examine the facts and look at both the good and bad decisions that the governing coalition had made over the last twenty years. And we weren't afraid to say what these decisions were.

Perhaps the social history of my generation doesn't make an enormous difference at an individual level, but when you form a collective and create as big a social movement as we did, the effect becomes exponential. It allows for a certain irreverence that emboldens us and deepens the level of criticism against the political decisions that were taken by the Concertación, the coalition that governed for the past twenty years.

The system of higher education in Chile had not undergone reform in three decades. Even the least socially conscious among us realized that, after thirty years, it was time for a change. Our first step was to figure out how best to communicate what we already knew, so we worked with a communications agency to help us to simplify our message. It took a lot of work to find a phrase or sentiment that would trigger the first protests. We needed to tap into what in Chile we would refer to as the "Jesuit sense of guilt" of the upper classes and make people question why they are deserving of this privilege and others are not. The goal was to prompt people to ask themselves, "Why do I have this privilege of access to education?" Conversely, we had to make the less fortunate feel anger, impotence, and frustration with an unfair system, and we had to show them that they received less not because they weren't good enough but because the deck was already stacked against them.

In thinking about these two very different groups with whom we had to build an emotional connection, we formulated simple messages around three elements of higher education. The first concerned the inequality of access to higher education. This was very easy to explain: among Chile's poorest 10 percent, two out of every ten people enter university; among the richest 10 percent, that number increases to nine out of ten. Along the way, for various reasons related to poverty, more poor people than rich people drop out of college, which makes graduation even more unequal. And it goes without saying that the poorest people in Chile rarely have the opportunity to attend the best universities.

The second message had to do with financing, a topic which is also easy to make people understand. Here we had the help of institutions that aren't necessarily left-leaning, such as the OECD, which had been deeply critical of the privatization of higher education in Chile. It's widely known that much of the population is in debt, so it wasn't hard to generate empathy for millions of students struggling to pay their tuition fees and stay in college. How is it possible that the state doesn't pay for education and we have to go into debt? The state contributes a mere 0.5 percent of GDP to higher education, while families contribute 1.8 percent. This is scandalous.

The third message had to do with regulation. There was a general feeling that the public was being ripped off; the pitfalls of deregulation and profit making in education were starting to show. Families felt that their sons and daughters were graduating only to become erudite unemployed. In the 1970s and '80s, people who studied law had a seat of honor; now they had to fight for a place, and salaries were lower than expected. Ultimately, expectations weren't being fulfilled because of deregulation of supply, inferior universities, and the fact that much of education had become purely about making a profit.

We told the students we wanted to democratize education. We said: "You aren't only going to study; you are going to build a society." I don't know if the general public understood, but it made a lot of sense to the students, and to me.

The objective of our communication campaign was to call a march for May 12. This was all. But when people took to the streets, it had to be big. We made a Web page and produced a video that called for the recovery of public education. Our video had more than ten thousand hits.

About thirty thousand protesters came to that first march, which we considered a huge success. People were motivated. They felt like they were participating in something big. We laid bare an uncomfortable truth for many Chilean families. They felt and understood what we were saying, and it made them indignant.

By the next march later that month, we had forty thousand people, and then one hundred thousand, and then more than five hundred thousand in a protest that we organized in Parque O'Higgins. I have a photo of myself speaking there—a moment I am never going to forget. The crowds and the energy created a sense that we were doing something of real significance. I'm proud to have been there. It was a good feeling to know that we weren't inventing anything or selling people a bill of goods, but instead we were part of the enormous number of Chileans who said, "Enough is enough."

To this day, I'm still surprised by the energy of the people who take to the streets again and again for education. When many people feel that they are part of a movement, at the beginning that movement grows exponentially. The fact that the government made many errors, not least of which was having a Ministry of Education that owned a university for profit, made people go out in even greater numbers. Attempts to repress innocent students during the street demonstrations only served to further fuel the flames of indignation.

At the same time, similar movements were taking place in other countries. Although I don't think these other protests directly affected the student movement in Chile, this coinciding fact added a sense of being part of something more momentous and global. We felt like we were a part of something much bigger. But the movement would have happened regardless of what was happening in the rest of the world because, here in Chile, there was a specific problem with a diagnosis. Many people were affected, and it had to explode at some time.

What has most amazed me is how the movement, which began with students, has transcended its original goal and become about politics. Chile had always been seen as a model of development, as the "jaguar of Latin America," and we managed to jeopardize the foundation on which past governments had constructed this image. We were always told that seven of every ten students are first-generation college students, and that sounds really nice, but when you look deeper, you realize that more than half of these students enter the university already in debt, and for what? A third-rate education at a bad university? More than half drop out of college, and of those who manage to graduate, approximately two-thirds don't find work in the subject they studied. All of a sudden we were questioning all that we had been told about the triumphs of the education system and thinking that we had been cheated. And that's why people began to question our political system.

The result of all this activism followed a logical path. The government responded to our demands by saying, "We like their ideas, but we just don't have resources."

"What do you mean they are no resources?" we asked. "Of course there are! What about tax reform? What about copper, which today is being mined for almost nothing?"

We proposed that something be done about the sovereignty of our natural resources, because there is more than enough money in Chilean soil to make education free. The government accused us of being ideological because we were talking about things that weren't purely educational. The conflict went on, and according to a poll by the research firm Adimark, 80 percent of the public wanted changes, but the government didn't want to solve the problem.

We realized that the changes couldn't come from Congress either, because we were in a presidential regime. The politics of forced consensus between the two major political coalitions has reigned for years. We needed to deepen our democracy; we needed to make the government respond to the social majority and acknowledge that there was a real questioning of democracy as we know it. They accused us of becoming politicized. But I think the politicization of the movement was the best thing that could have happened to it. People should become even more politicized to clearly transmit the need for constitutional and tax reform, and to open spaces for mechanisms of referendum.

Our principle achievement was to stop the neoliberal agenda of the government in education. They announced some regulatory changes, and the debates that have been going on in Congress for three years have advanced somewhat. Today, there is finally a healthy debate over the role of for-profit universities, and the best students from the poorest 60 percent of the population will be eligible for government scholarships. This number is up from 40 percent. University financing is still a demand, as is the financing of primary education, but not only did we move the debate forward, we even changed its ideological parameters. Although this government doesn't want to cede ideologically, now academics and different political forces dare to consider different options. We have changed the realm of what is possible.

GREECE

OVERVIEW

In the last two years, Greece has become synonymous with economic failure and chaos. In the United States, its name is shorthand for the problems of irresponsible fiscal policy—by 2011 its public debt had exceeded 160 percent of GDP, the highest in Europe—and austerity hawks around the world have often held up the country as an example of what happens if deficits are not brought quickly under control. Until Greece received a partial bailout from the European Union in October, interest rates on Greek sovereign debt had grown shockingly high. Government bonds were demoted to junk status by ratings agencies. The country of 11 million had fiscal problems so complicated and intractable that they threatened to dismantle the euro. Four years after the beginning of the financial crisis, the economy was still estimated to be shrinking at an accelerating rate of 5 percent per annum. The legions of jobless were also growing at a steady and steep rate.

But while the most common story in the international media was that Greece was a grim example of excess, an out-of-control welfare state, and greedy pensioners, the reality was much more complicated. For one, Greek government spending, though higher than that of many other countries, seemed sustainable during the boom years before the financial crisis, when the economy was growing at a healthy clip. It proved not to be—but that wasn't just a miscalculation of the Greek government in particular, but more generally a failure of economics and the economic framework that Europe, and much of the world, had adopted. Unfettered markets, it was believed, would lead to efficient and stable outcomes, with high growth and shared prosperity. The financial crisis that nailed all the other countries took an especially exacting toll on Greece, where the economy had grown partially dependent on tourism. When wealthier Europeans saw their savings slashed in the markets, cutting back on luxuries like a Greek summer holiday was one of the easiest decisions.

Most egregiously, though, many of Greece's problems were a direct result of taking staggeringly bad advice from American bankers—among them, the same ones that propped up the mighty, dangerous bubble of the 2000s. When the bubble broke, Greece suffered two crises: the broader one, and its own. One Wall Street bank engineered a scheme in which the Mediterranean country could hide its ballooning debt with derivatives—the same instruments that bankers on Wall Street abused with such devastating consequences in profiting from the subprime mortgage market. The deception may have helped Greece abide by deficit rules in place for European Union countries, and when combined with other deceptions of Greece's statistical agency, may have enabled some politicians to cling to office a bit longer. The cost was a crisis somewhat delayed but massively amplified, as confidence in Greece seemed to evaporate with the exposure of the deceptions.

But the notion that all would have been well if only Greece had stuck to the rules—kept its deficit below 3 percent of GDP and its debt below 60 percent of GDP—was put to the lie by what happened in Spain and Ireland, both countries that were given A+ grades for obeying the rules. They had surpluses, not deficits; they had low debt-to-GDP ratios. But they, like Greece, were hit by the tidal wave of recession that came from across the Atlantic.

Surpluses quickly turned into massive deficits, and small debt-to-GDP ratios soon turned into high ones.

It's small wonder then that outrage began to grasp many Greeks as their living standards eroded, the promise of a prosperous future began to evaporate, and their European neighbors balked at rescuing the drowning economy—and then demanded harsh sacrifices in exchange. Greeks began taking to the streets. In May 2011, taking a cue from Spaniards who had successfully staged mass demonstrations, the Greek *indignados* were born.

Like the Spaniards they emulated and the Americans who would follow, the Greek protesters had a variety of demands. What seemed to unite them was a sense that the formal political system had failed them and that the only way to reclaim the national dialogue was to take direct action. As Antonis Voulgarelis writes, "Voters don't trust anyone anymore." It was time to take matters into their own hands.

NO TEARS FOR GREEK DEMOCRACY

Fivos Papahadjis

Fivos Papahadjis, thirty-seven, is a freelance illustrator and graphic artist. His interests include comics, graphic design, and music. He lives and works in Athens.

It's been thirty-seven years since the downfall of the military regime and the beginning of the post-dictatorship period in Greece. It just so happens I am thirty-seven years old.

I was born and raised in the center of Athens, where I have witnessed the often turbulent history of modern Greek politics unfold through its protests and rallies, sometimes even from my own balcony overlooking one of the central avenues of the Greek capital. Protests and violent clashes with the police are not uncommon here. I can remember as a young boy being driven to school past the still smoking rubble of the previous night's riots a number of times. I have seen crowds gather for the customary pre-election rallies of the big political parties; in recent times I have even heard the speeches of their leaders and would-be prime ministers from inside my living room.

The course of my life runs parallel to the period in which Greece, wounded by the seven-year-long dictatorship, has been striving to catch up with the rest of the world and establish its position in the European family as a stable democratic partner and a reliable ally. The conservative and socialist governments of the period succeeded in making Greece a member of the European Economic Community (EEC). They managed to include the country in the core of the advanced economies that would be able to participate in the first common European currency, the euro. As a crowning achievement, Athens successfully organized the 2004 Olympic Games.

Over the years, the demonstrations outside my window started to shrink in magnitude, lacking the enthusiasm of the huge rallies of the 1980s and early 1990s and slowly giving way to televised debates. Despite the occasional petrol bomb, things were relatively quiet by Greek standards, with the exception of the December 2008 riots, which were in response to the death of a teenager who was shot by a policeman. For the well-informed, the economic chaos that followed that period of false prosperity may have been no big news. Greece had been living on borrowed EU money for decades with increasingly incompetent and corrupt governments failing to invest that money on necessary infrastructure.

But the cracks were starting to show. With one political scandal succeeding the other, the global financial crisis hit Greece with full force. The Panhellenic Socialist Movement (PASOK) socialist party government under Prime Minister George Papandreou had won the October 2009 elections on the promise that money would be found to lead the country out of the crisis. Needless to say, that promise was not kept. After the decision to induct Greece into the IMF, drastic austerity measures were announced with alarming frequency.

In hindsight, the spring of 2011 was a gloomy, pessimistic season, full of bad news and anxious conversations. Debates and discussions were heard all over the city. More and more people were talking politics instead of the usual football and showbiz gossip. It was evident that the tension was getting to more or less everyone and that irritated Greeks would not require much of an excuse to speak their minds.

I was notified of the May 25 demonstration via Facebook, and I spread the message like thousands of others did over those three or four days. It's not clear who sent the first message or why that overwhelming chain of messages got all those people out in the streets on that particular day. After all, smaller groups had started demonstrating the week before. One thing is clear, that we were inspired and encouraged by the movements in Northern Africa and Spain. Rumor had it that the Spanish put up a sign reading, "Quiet or we'll wake up the Greeks." When I got to Syntagma (Constitution) Square, the place opposite the Greek parliament where the crowd had gathered, a huge Spanish flag dominated all other protest banners. With bold black letters on it was written in Spanish: "We have awakened. What time is it? It's time they went home!"

I'm not really the demonstration-going type. I had only attended a couple of anti-war marches in the past, protesting against the invasion of Iraq by NATO forces. I am not a member of any political party, and I felt at ease with these people who were holding no party banners—no red, black, blue, or green flags. A few of them only had a Greek flag. The rest of us held our hands in the air and with open palms aimed at the parliament in a typical Greek gesture of discontent. There we were, with thousands of hands, a sea of hands up in the air with open palms and thousands of people from different backgrounds, of different ages, chanting, "Thieves! Thieves!" and "Take your measures and get out!"

Almost immediately, I ran into some friends and then some more. The mood was celebratory; the rage against rotten politicians was expressed in humorous chants and handmade picket signs. In parts of the square, some people had already set up tents and hammocks to camp right there, opposite the parliament. It was surreal! As if the entire beach of a Greek island had been teleported from the Aegean directly into the heart of Athens.

People were walking around Syntagma Square between the campers, some enjoying a chilled can of beer, others sitting down in circles and smoking a joint, others trying to organize a basic infirmary tent. It was like a festival, a great get-together of the Greek citizens who had finally decided to stop watching and start acting. Before long I was on all fours, drawing a cartoon pig (a reference to the P.I.I.G. countries: Portugal, Ireland, Italy, and Greece) on a white sheet of cloth, and I was surrounded by people commenting on the drawing and making suggestions.

A meeting was being held in the lower part of the square, with anyone willing to take the stand and make a brief statement respectfully heard by the audience. In turn, people raised hands, taking a vote on any matter that needed to be decided there and then. More experienced speakers gave the stand to people who had clearly never addressed an audience before in their lives but felt compelled to step forward to express their anger, or simply their excitement to be there. Some of them were students; some were pensioners. It was almost like a small parliament with the exception that this one seemed to be more in touch with reality and the will of the people than the real one across the street.

Late at night, the majority had gone home, vowing to continue the following day and the day after that, until the austerity measures had been recalled or the government had stepped down. And Athens was not the only place in Greece where rallies were held, with citizens occupying central town spots and protesting. It was happening in every corner of my country, way beyond the earshot of my apartment balcony.

The next day the crowd gathered again. Waves of people surfaced from the Syntagma underground metro station, uniting with the ever-swelling crowd on the square. The Greek flags had multiplied, and the crowd was even more diverse. A band was playing samba, and some people were dancing while others were hitting empty pots and pans Argentine-style. A new banner had taken its place next to the Spanish one: "Quiet or we'll wake up the French!"

Every night, more protesters occupied Syntagma and other spots across Greece. The square was covered in tents and banners for more than two months, with crowds ranging from ten thousand to forty thousand people, depending on the day of the week, and exceeding one hundred fifty thousand on the days of general strikes. Sunday gatherings were especially numerous and coincided with weekly protests of so-called "indignants" in various European cities. Nearby fast food shops and cafés had never seen better days!

The square transformed into its own miniature city. Over time it became evident that there were two main rallying points on the site. The so-called "upper" square, where protesters chanted slogans against government, journalists, and the entire political system, and the "lower" square, where the tents were set up and the daily assembly took place. Athenians would debate politics in the birthplace of democracy under the shadow of the Acropolis just as they had done in ancient times. It made the process even more symbolic and exciting in my eyes, especially in light of one recurring theme—need for a more direct democratic system.

Fortunately, nationalistic ideas were not voiced in the assembly, although they were probably left in the minds of some flag bearers in the "upper" square. Instead, many immigrants took the microphone and were warmly applauded. Volunteers were organized into groups that took care of practical problems like keeping the place clean and providing food for the campers, legal support, or first aid. We used whatever we had, including a ladder for a stretcher. A Web site was also launched, and the installation of a microphone and speakers made everyone's work easier.

Meanwhile, inside the parliament it was business as usual. The government was getting ready to pass new measures with MPs (members of parliament) starting to worry about the perseverance of the protests—increasingly so after they had to be ushered out of the building by police under the cover of darkness and through the nearby National Garden. They were desperate to avoid confronting the now-agitated crowd, which was calling for the "brothel of a parliament" to be "set on fire."

A few days later, Prime Minister Papandreou was on the verge of resigning, with more than one hundred fifty thousand people surrounding the House of Parliament. The crowd's aim was to blockade the building and stop the MPs from entering and giving their vote of confidence to the government. It was the first time that the, until then, cool-and-collected police used tear gas to hold back the protesters. Small and random groups of self-proclaimed anarchists attacked the police, which the police in turn used as an excuse to spray enormous amounts of chemicals and attack the main body of peaceful protesters. The result was seventy wounded on both sides.

Have you ever been teargassed? Have you even smelled tear gas from a distance? I was sprayed flat on the chest, from point blank range. I tried not to breathe in, but I was in a cloud of the stuff. My eyes started stinging and burning while the smell of pepper and chlorine scalded the inside of my nose and mouth. It was as if I was breathing in fire, and I couldn't keep my watering eyes open even for a second to see where I was going as I heard people shouting and running all around me. I sat down and raised my hands over my head in an attempt to show that I was not in a position to threaten the riot police now running toward me in full gear and gas masks. I felt my arm being grabbed, and I was dragged across the asphalt and out of the way by a policeman.

As I lay by the pavement, spitting and trying to regain my sight, someone gave me water. I washed my eyes, and a reaction with the chemicals made the stinging even worse. The water was literally burning my skin. It took about five minutes before I was fit to get up and walk again, defeated but proud. Despite the heavy use of tear gas and violence by the police, the majority of the demonstrators remained at the spot until late at night and returned the next afternoon, and the day after that. We had lost the battle but not the war.

Camped in Syntagma Square for two weeks, members of the movement, if one could call it that, demanded that the government recall the austerity measures. We insisted that those responsible for the economic scandals be brought to justice and that the embezzled money be returned and used to pay for Greece's debt. A banner proclaimed Papandreou to be the IMF's employee of the year, while another said, "They're not incompetent, they are traitors." By now, some people in the crowd were waving mini-gallows.

Other movements in smaller cities began to wither away, with the exception of Thessaloniki, but Athens was still going strong. Perhaps we had Loukanikos, or Sausage, the riot dog, to thank for that. A stray mutt who first wandered his way into street protests a few years ago, Loukanikos has been at the helm of all the demonstrations since. The fearless and friendly canine became the unofficial mascot of the indignants and earned countless international press mentions.

For the next couple of weeks, activity seemed to be slowing down, with reports from Brussels announcing tax increases to ensure Greece would receive the next installment of European financial aid. Skirmishes between police and small groups of hooded youths would flare up sporadically, and signs suggested that the stage for the final confrontation was being set for June 29, when the new measures were to be ratified. A two-day general strike was proclaimed to paralyze the country and oppose the impending austerity cuts.

That day almost two hundred thousand people showed up, and many came early in the morning to attempt to storm the metal wall installed by the police so that MPs could reach the parliament and vote. Among them was my sixty-seven-year-old father, who felt partly responsible for having supported one of the major political parties involved in derailing the country. The crowd was on the same scale as the majestic political rallies of the 1980s that I had witnessed as a child! As we had done for the past month, men and women of all ages and social status, some holding their children, demonstrated peacefully by clapping hands and chanting slogans.

Early in the afternoon the by-now-familiar group of youths clad in black and wearing hoods and masks launched an attack against the heavily armed riot squad that guarded the far side of the House of Parliament, about 200 meters away from where we stood. The hissing sound of the tear gas canisters flying between our feet and the silhouettes of masked riot police running toward us through the chemical fog is what I remember next. Blinded by a cocktail of different types of tear gas that made it very difficult to breathe, I grabbed my father, and crouching under the toxic cloud, we headed for the nearest metro entrance where we were hoping for a gasp of air. Those were the longest thirty seconds of my life! On our way down the stairs, one of many volunteers sprayed our faces with a solution of water and Maalox, the indigestion medicine, with surprisingly soothing results. Bless her, wherever she is!

What followed can be compared to wild nature documentaries when packs of predatory animals attack a herd of antelopes. The brutality of the police response was unprecedented. On the square that was turned into a gas chamber, only the treetops were visible. The asphyxiating crowd was coughing and trying to breathe through their scarves and T-shirts. Their faces white from the Maalox solution and their eyes red, they were setting fire to garbage cans in an attempt to create smoke and disperse the tear gas. The police were chasing people indiscriminately all over the center of Athens for hours, beating them, throwing stun grenades, and spraying literally tons of dangerous and in some cases expired chemicals. Even after it was announced that the bill had passed by a narrow majority, thousands of people remained at the square chanting, "Bread! Education! Freedom! The Junta didn't end in 1973."

Despite dramatic calls from the hospital tent doctors to stop the chemical warfare, the police were only too eager to make clear that no one was to set foot on the square again. They were cracking heads open left and right and spraying tear gas inside the underground metro station. Policemen riding on motorbikes even attacked un-suspecting tourists eating in a nearby tourist spot! While the usual couple of hundred hooded hooligans vandalized the center without being arrested, hundreds of citizens and fifty policemen were being rushed to the hospital, either wounded or suffering from serious respiratory problems. Miraculously, nobody died.

Things were never the same for the indignants, though. The following day, a few thousand assembled again in front of the parliament in a courageous act of defiance. The temperature had started to rise, and Athenian summers can be very hot. The air still had the stench of the last day's battle. The square was in ruins, but tents were being set up yet again. Even though the bill had been passed, even after that chilling display of police brutality, there were people determined to stay there until the embezzled money was returned and those responsible were behind bars.

For the entire month of July, rallies were held daily on the square by ever-diminishing crowds, until a police operation swept the indignants' camp on August 1, on the pretext of public hygiene concerns. It was over. Or was it?

On October 28, an annual commemoration of Greek involvement in World War II, thousands of citizens gathered all across the country and prevented the military parades from starting until all politicians had abandoned the scene. Fear of public outcry led several members of the ruling party to publicly question Papandreou's policies, especially after his announcement of a referendum on whether Greece should revert to its previous monetary system of the drachma, to the great irritation of European leaders. That lack of confidence led to the formation of a new coalition government under the former Vice President of the European Central Bank, Lucas Papademos, who was entrusted to secure the next installment of European aid and lead the country to elections as soon as possible.

Of course, it is too early to estimate the influence that the indignants' movement may have had in the bigger picture of things to come. Even though the popular assemblies were forced out of Syntagma, they are now blossoming in squares all across Greece. Naïve as we may have been, our movement became a model of persistence. We proved that the people can get things done. We showed that we can come together under no party banners and intervene when we feel betrayed by our representatives. We demonstrated that, from now on, further flogging of the Greek lower and middle classes will not go unopposed.

My country is in the eye of the storm that many say is a financial world war. Any predictions would be senseless from my part. But somewhere in the camaraderie displayed on Syntagma Square, on the Maalox-splashed white faces of my compatriots, I'd like to think I caught a glimpse of the future.

NIGHTS IN SYNTAGMA SQUARE

Antonis Voulgarelis

Antonis Voulgarelis, twenty-three, was born in Athens and studied communications and public relations at Corfu Technical University, graduating in September 2011. He currently works as an intern for the Agricultural Bank of Greece. He has been a member of the Indignados of Athens movement since its inception in May 2011.

In May 2011 Syntagma Square in central Athens became the nexus of three months of protests against the Greek government, austerity measures, a deepening recession, and a proclaimed surrender of sovereignty by the government to the IMF and the European Union. The movement began through social media, specifically Facebook. I first learned about it through the "Indignados of Athens" page, named after the protests in Spain, which had started ten days earlier. I was invited to the group by one of my best friends who had heard about it on the Internet. I attended its first day, May 25, and found myself among people of different backgrounds and ages: students, pensioners, the unemployed, young people, and children. The second day I went back.

The movement took a more dynamic form and was further empowered and structured after two or three days. We started organizing informal debates on social issues, the economy, and education. We disapproved of the unfair taxation system, the quality of education and our institutions, and the quality of life. We challenged the credibility of our political system. I had never participated in a social movement before, with the exception of the march against the war in Iraq in March 2003, when I was sixteen years old. But this time it was different.

I believed in this movement. It seemed to be a moment when the world was changing. An entire political system was being turned upside down. Our movement across Europe and around the world sent a clear message: the political system does not get a second chance because in its current form it doesn't represent us, the real people.

The initial one hundred protesters gradually rose to two hundred, and the two hundred rose to three hundred. The movement eventually gained popular support, mobilizing thousands of people who might have never participated in such activism before. On Sunday nights, tens of thousands of people came down to Syntagma Square and joined their voices with ours. I stayed at the square in a tent for three months. I didn't sleep there every night, but I did stay for most of the time.

My personal problems were serious at that point. My father was unemployed, and my mother was sick. I was still a student, a senior in college, but I abstained from classes in order to stay at the square. I came to view my own troubles in a broader social context rather than a personal one. I had struggled to finish my college education, and I felt that I ought to fight this battle at Syntagma. I owed it to my family, who had helped me pay for college. Even though money was tight, I managed to finish my degree and finally graduate in September 2011. But I went down to Syntagma for all my friends who had to quit college because they couldn't afford it.

We organized ourselves by setting up various groups: a communications team, an artistic team that arranged theater and music performances, a cleaning team, and a catering crew. Following discussions every night, we listened to music played by the different groups. There was a very optimistic spirit, something that had been so badly missing in Greek society.

Spending lots of time in the same place with people gave me the chance to interact with those that I didn't have the opportunity to meet or chat with in my daily life. We talked a lot, we got to know each other better; some of us even lived in the same neighborhood but had never met before. I met people on the entire political spectrum at Syntagma: the leftist, conservative, and apolitical. The mix was extremely interesting. The time I spent there helped me develop my critical skills, to incorporate diverse thoughts into my political thinking. This is why I stayed there for so long. It was history in the making; I wanted to be part of it. I wanted to question, to challenge, to discuss.

The nights were very hot, particularly during a heat wave that hit Athens in July. The shopkeepers of the restaurant chains around Syntagma Square helped by giving us food and water.

On June 15, nearly twenty-five thousand additional protesters descended upon Syntagma Square, as Parliament was voting on a new package of austerity measures so that the country could raise €6.4 billion and continue receiving funding from Greece's year-old €110 billion international bailout. The square seemed to sink from the burst of indignation coming from all citizens, regardless of age, social background, or voting behavior. I saw parents with young children who were complaining for their children's future, which was undermined by the actions of the current government.

The riot police were extremely violent; we were trapped in Syntagma Square under a suffocating atmosphere of tear gas thrown at us from different directions. I saw middle-age people with white faces from homemade remedies that contained Maalox, offered by fellow protesters to tolerate the attacks. But they did not leave. They gave us courage, pleading, "Stay here. We have to remain in our seats. We have to fight and defend our cause." The authorities didn't succeed in suppressing us; on the contrary, we stayed, we organized ourselves, and our solidarity has shown results. According to news reports, fifteen hundred police clashed with protesters, and thirty-six police and thirty civilians were injured during the riots that lasted several hours.

That was a spontaneous moment for us, which the entire planet saw through television and the Internet. I watched the world's biggest media outlets covering the events from the rooftop of Athens Plaza Hotel at Syntagma. It was realtime—history in the making. I uploaded pictures from my smart phone to my Facebook account, where my 2,200 friends could follow tweets, status updates, and photos of the events at Syntagma. This day of clashes, and the perseverance we showed, made me believe that Greece can change and that Europe can change—that our movement can bring a new dynamic, which the political elites were not expecting and didn't know how to tackle.

Our occupation ended when municipal police removed us from Syntagma Square on the night of August 7. Now I stay in touch with the people I met during that time. We chat through Facebook, and we often meet at the square. We talk about how this movement will evolve, and we continue discussing the country's troubles. We also talk about further steps. Social networks are a double-edged sword. They can either strengthen a movement or undermine it if different interest groups destroy its momentum using lies or negative messages. But their power is tremendous. They can spread the word in seconds. Months after the protests in my country ended, I followed the news from Occupy Wall Street on Facebook and Twitter.

The movement was not only a political protest. It was a social and economic protest. The European elite were unable to comply with society's demands. And the world was shaken due to this profound economic crisis. Madrid's movement, the one initiated at Plaza de Sol shortly before the Greek protests, prompted the rest of Europe to participate, causing a domino effect throughout the continent and of course across the Atlantic, with the Occupy Wall Street movement. The message is clear: we must all stay united, and we mustn't back down. The meaning of these movements is one: to take our lives into our own hands.

The main accomplishment of our movement was the fall of the Papandreou government. This was unprecedented in Greece's modern history. George Papandreou's resignation as prime minister in November 2011 showed the pressure that this spontaneous political movement put on the political landscape—from an independent movement that wasn't organized by trade unions or by the left.

The government collapsed under pressure from frustrated citizens who decided to take matters into their own hands. I am glad to see people becoming stronger and believing more in themselves—empowerment that was achieved by the protests.

The world is changing everywhere. There is a dire need for people to revise some of the things hitherto taken for granted. As movements around the globe take hold, they bring hope to societies and form a common front against the political elites who have lost touch with voters. In Greece, this will be reflected at the next election. We no longer have confidence in a system that collapses. I think the vote will be directed at no one and that the rate of abstention will go beyond expectation because voters don't trust anyone anymore.

The *indignados* of Athens movement changed me dramatically and transformed me into an active citizen. In May 2011 the dilemma for me was "sofa and Facebook versus tent and Syntagma." The second alternative won by far, and the results are obvious. Our problems in Greece resemble cholera epidemics. We knew that the problems of the person sitting next to us would soon become our problems. This realization played a significant role in shaping the movement. Everyone realized that our economy was sinking, and people had to readjust their comfort level.

Following the fall of the Papandreou government, I can say I am quite optimistic. I sense that we have overcome the first step of the problem. The Papandreou government was disastrous for our country, and its collapse was the outcome of a tremendous social reaction, a reaction that stated, "We exceeded our limits."

OCCUPY WALL STREET

OVERVIEW

The real surprise about the Occupy Wall Street movement is probably that it didn't happen earlier. In the 2000s, the United States had been through a gauntlet of economic and political disappointments that rivaled almost any in its history. First, in the wake of the tragedy of September 11, President George W. Bush launched two wars—one of questionable utility in Afghanistan, to root out the Taliban, and the other in Iraq, now regarded as a colossal mistake by a huge number of Americans. The conflicts left thousands of Americans (and far more Afghans and Iraqis) dead, but the second shock was the price tag. Wars originally pitched to the public as having a price tag of a few billion dollars by end of decade were on pace to cost the country $4 trillion or more. Rather than being paid for with taxes, like most wars, the adventures in Iraq and Afghanistan were put on the nation's credit card. And in the midst of it all, Bush insisted on huge tax cuts that heavily benefited the wealthiest Americans.

If not many people seemed to care, it was probably because the wars were not the only thing the country was putting on the charge card. Cheap credit masked fundamental economic problems. Banks marketed subprime mortgages to buyers who could barely afford a down payment. Skyrocketing real estate prices meant middle-class Americans could borrow against their houses to finance splurges and expensive necessities alike. And why not? House prices, it seemed, could only go up. But the truth was that Americans were not getting much richer at all. The median income of American households stagnated through the decade, never regaining the peak it climbed to before the dot-com bust. Savings rates were at all-time lows.

A storm was brewing on the horizon, but few people understood that it was going to be a Category 5 financial hurricane. The overheated housing market was only part of the problem. Wall Street banks had used new credit instruments—credit default swaps, derivatives, and other over-the-counter transactions barely understood by the mathematicians who invented them—to leverage the risks they took to astronomical heights, which equaled astronomical profits. Through it all, Wall Street benefited from one of the most lax financial regulatory environments in recent history. It was getting hard to tell the regulators and the government officials from the bankers.

The big banks claimed that, with all that leveraging, they were actually spreading the risk nice and thin. When the housing bubble collapsed at the end of 2007, it turned out they were indeed spreading the risk—nice and thick, into every corner of America and the world. It was a bust on steroids. Some of the more overextended outfits—Bear Stearns, Lehman Brothers—collapsed, but the fact was that most of the banks were "too big to fail." Led by the Treasury Department, Congress initiated a $700 billion bailout. In the panic of the crash, those who complained that it was a no-strings-attached cash transfer to the very entities that had caused the crisis were brushed aside. The U.S. government was willing to do anything to stabilize the collapsing markets.

As the grim pieces fell around them, Americans struggled to make sense of their new economic reality. The economy was in deep recession. Retirement funds were lost, as were homes, with alarming frequency. The unemployment rate lurched upwards, heading to 10.6 percent before stabilizing around 9 percent, a "new normal" that was a serious drag on the economy. Americans' tax money had been used to save the unscrupulous banks and bankers—who were still raking in bonuses by the billions—but they were still stuck with their old debts. Inequality reached historic levels. Meanwhile, the country needed help from the government more than ever, but public finances were in disarray. Tax receipts were down anyway, and since deficits had been used to finance the expensive wars, accounts were far more overdrawn than they should have been. Worst of all, the politicians who were supposed to be leading the country out of the woods were either ineffective, beholden to special interests, or in thrall to fantasies about economic policy that the crisis should have long destroyed.

Finally, there was rage. At first inchoate, it gradually coalesced into a particular perspective: the American people had been screwed by their government, their regulators, and most of all Wall Street. It might have ended there, but then something magnificent happened. Halfway around the world, activists with seemingly much more insurmountable problems had shown that mass action could create change. With Tahrir and Tunis as inspirations, Americans who might have sunk into apathy rallied together: they were off to occupy Wall Street and confront the powerful and unscrupulous financial elites on their own turf.

Beginning on September 17, 2011, protesters started filling Zuccotti Park in the heart of New York's financial district. What was at first a trickle of people with uncertain aims mushroomed into a movement of tens and then hundreds of thousands. In New York and many other cities—Los Angeles, Oakland, and Philadelphia, to name a few—they marched under the banner "We are the 99 percent."

FROM WISCONSIN TO WALL STREET: A CHEESEHEAD DOES NOT STAND ALONE

Harry Waisbren

Harry Waisbren is a co-founder of the Job Party and a social media analyst. He is an ardent supporter of both the Wisconsin uprising and Occupy Wall Street, as well as a proud Wisconsinite and New York City transplant.

I'm proud of my Wisconsin heritage including the silly hats called "cheeseheads." This foam rubber headgear shaped like a wedge of cheddar cheese is worn by fans of Wisconsin's beloved Green Bay Packers football team. Cheeseheads are pretty absurd looking, but because they are so recognizable they are now a symbol of progressive Wisconsin values and a prop for protesters who want to show their solidarity with like-minded individuals.

It was April 26th, 2011, and I could hardly believe I was breathing the same air as some of the most influential activists in the Arab Spring. Just that afternoon I'd received an e-mail announcing that two of the founding members of the Egyptian revolution's April 6 Youth Movement—Ahmed Maher and Waleed Rashed—were in town on a press tour. What they really wanted, though, was to meet with young American bloggers and activists. So there

I was with about thirty other New York City activists, ready to discuss revolutionary tactics in the digital age. Yet I was in awe and unable to speak, overwhelmed with gratitude for how these brave Egyptians had inspired my home state of Wisconsin to fight back in a manner I would have previously thought impossible. The meeting felt historically momentous, and indeed it was. A season later, many of these same New York activists would leverage such inspiration once again through Occupy Wall Street.

I first moved to New York City in August 2010 in search of opportunity, despite its being the only place this Midwestern boy thought would be too much to handle on a permanent basis. Little did I know what this move to the big city would hold for me, not to mention the connections this movement would create between Wisconsin and my newly adopted home of New York. Recognizing and facilitating the reciprocal inspiration between these two places has already become the pride of my life and a mission I am ardently committed to upholding.

Reciprocal inspiration is a concept I came up with after studying Wael Ghonim's work during the Egyptian revolution. Ghonim is the Google marketing executive who anonymously administered the "We are all Khaled Said" Facebook page that acted as a central hub for online organizing. A key aspect of his social media strategy is to use it to inspire readers to break past the "psychological barrier" that prevents them from taking action in the streets. But I realized it doesn't stop there because those taking part in these barrier-breaking actions could further inspire others, even those who took action in the first place. Social media makes this possible in a way that is unprecedented, and that is game changing.

This is why I felt a duty to defend Occupy Wall Street on that crucial October 14 morning, along with so many others. New York mayor Michael Bloomberg had made his move to shut the nascent effort down despite (or because of) the burgeoning mobilization it had spawned. But more than two thousand of us were standing side by side before the dawn when the eviction was to come, waiting for the wrath of Wall Street to descend through their police proxies. All I could think about were those faced with the same decision during the Wisconsin occupation in Madison earlier in the year. The occupiers in Madison set a powerful example by persevering under similar straits. They were willing and able to hold the state capitol and maintain the movement, even in the face of Governor Scott Walker discussing inserting agent provocateurs and threatening to sic the National Guard on them. Their courage was why I knew I had to stand strong for Occupy Wall Street, despite my fears that all hell would break loose. Come what may, it was worth it, if only so we could further inspire others, like those who inspired us.

We held our positions, and deafening cheers erupted when word came that Mayor Bloomberg backed down and we had won. People were so excited that the message couldn't even make it through the reflecting chorus of the "people's mic," as the human echo chamber that we used as our main means of communication came to be known. The people's mic then announced that "One of the most beautiful aspects of this movement is the solidarity," a fact that was proven beyond a shadow of a doubt the next day when solidarity rallies were organized across the planet for #Occupy (the # is a reference to the Twitter hashtag to delineate the effort's social media parlance). The ABC news ticker right above us at the Times Square rally was actively reporting on how "Occupy Wall Street Goes Worldwide." We roared each time it ran across the screen.

This rapid response, this explosion of worldwide goodwill and support, was only possible through an adrenaline-powered leap over so many psychological barriers. Social media makes this happen in a completely new way, allowing inspiring actions across the globe to almost instantaneously boomerang back around and persuade others to act. The vast spread of Occupy Wall Street solidarity efforts throughout the fall of 2011 is one instance of this, as well as the similar support from across the country for the Wisconsin occupation that past spring.

The Wisconsin uprising began on February 11, after the governor declared war on government workers by attempting to unilaterally remove the right for public unions to collectively bargain. But he did not understand the depth of Wisconsin's progressive heritage, which combined with inspiration from the ongoing Egyptian revolution, would spark a fight back that would ignite the hopes of the country. Things first came to a head on February 14, when protests began outside the capitol building in Madison, and then they escalated the next day when protesters began occupying the interior. I was following these events as closely as I could, and, just like the Egyptians, found that Twitter was the perfect place to get on-the-ground reports in real time. I had spent years as a student activist dreaming of this kind of mobilization, and Twitter's ability to centralize these reports through a hashtag, #WIunion, allowed me to keep a grasp on it despite not being there to revel in the moment.

A few weeks prior I had become a co-founder of a new political organization called the Job Party, and we decided to launch officially in tandem with the burgeoning Wisconsin uprising. We committed to do all we could to galvanize solidarity for the effort in general as it fit directly with our mission to be the progressive counter to the Tea Party. The Job Party is not a political party per se. Rather, our focus is like the Tea Party's in terms of using media-savvy grassroots action to change the political narrative— away from the distraction of how we are "taxed enough already" (the T-E-A in Tea Party), and onto the real problem of how we need jobs.

Wisconsin was under attack from its Tea Party governor, and collectively the state was crying out, "Enough!" Even though my commitments in New York prevented me from physically being in Wisconsin, the Job Party became the perfect platform for me to help defend my home state against this official declaration of class war on working families made by Walker and the Tea Party.

Back in New York we acted quickly, and by February 18, we held one of the first Wisconsin solidarity rallies that would soon sweep the nation. What followed was the realization of just how powerful the reciprocal inspiration boomerang could be, as we witnessed our "Cheesehead Rallies" grow exponentially in size and energy. We wore cheeseheads newly shipped from Wisconsin to symbolize our solidarity, relishing the opportunity to follow their example.

A catalyzing point was already reached by our second rally on the 22nd, in which participants broke past their psychological barriers *en masse*. I watched as cynicism and learned helplessness evaporated in light of the powerful precedent being set. Wisconsinites were fighting back no holds barred, and the occupation in Madison had made my home state a light for all of us in New York and beyond to follow out of the abyss.

The escalation of our rallies inspired MoveOn.org in particular to call for Wisconsin events at the capitols of all fifty states. The organization used it as an opportunity to launch the meta-brand American Dream movement rhetoric prescribed by progressive organizer Van Jones, and it committed from the outset to the example Wisconsin occupiers were setting. We worked hand in hand with MoveOn to organize a focal point City Hall rally for the nationwide Day of Action on the 26th. This national outpouring of support upped the ante in Wisconsin, where the momentum helped the marches break the threshold of one hundred thousand participants in the low-population state.

The best part of all of this for me was when I heard from activist friends and colleagues back home who had seen me on TV or in other media. They were genuinely exhilarated and astonished to find out that anyone was even paying attention to Wisconsin. Indeed, the media environment of New York gave us added capacity to bring the fight into the national consciousness. We were having a tangible impact on the ground in Madison, despite our physical distance. Showing such appreciation here helped provide an increasingly persuasive rationale for more Wisconsinites to break past their psychological barriers and hit the streets, and I realized in turn that I had a special role to play as a Wisconsin emissary in New York.

Social media allows for word to spread about activism swiftly and widely like never before. The inspiring example from these actions also leads to this boomerang effect, which can plant seeds in the minds of those who would like to follow in the footsteps of other activist movements. We saw this dynamic play out in the vast solidarity from the Wisconsin capitol occupation, and from these easily spreadable seeds of inspiration I see a direct line to the mass support in America for Occupy Wall Street.

The clearest evidence of this pattern could be seen in the way the Wisconsin occupation moved outside and onto the lawn in front of the capitol building to form a tent city called "Walkerville." The name of this occupation was a reference to its inspiration from the Depression-era Hooverville tent city. Walkerville began in the thick of winter, even before Governor Walker had successfully shut out the would-be occupiers, and constituted a final push to expose the nihilistic nature of his state budget proposal. Social media reports quickly provided a model for a parallel occupation in New York called "Bloombergville," an occupation that was similarly set up in proximity to City Hall. As in the case of Walkerville, it was premised on preventing the drastic cuts that the mayor had proposed in the city budget.

I came by with a flipcam and a few of the cheeseheads we used for our solidarity rallies and filmed Bloombergville residents thanking Wisconsinites while wearing the hats. I was both surprised and encouraged by how much the Bloombergville protesters wanted to acknowledge the activists at Walkerville for inspiring their action, and what followed was a textbook example of reciprocal inspiration. I distributed these videos online to activists on the ground in Wisconsin through Twitter and the local blog Dane101.com.

Dane101 and Wisconsin activists in turn organized response videos of Walkerville participants thanking Bloombergville residents for inspiring them back, which I distributed locally through the Job Party blog and Twitter again. To show their respect and appreciation for activists at Bloombergville, the Wisconsin protesters even donned Statue of Liberty hats!

Sure, the head-wear was "cheesy," but its impact on the solidarity and confidence of protesters on far-flung sides of the country was profound. After the appreciation-filled introduction, we organized a Skype video chat between all of us so that we could share tactics and strategy. This kind of support emboldened the small group on that loud and dirty New York City street corner, making participants feel much less isolated. The connection helped them realize they were having an impact that was much greater than they could physically see.

How much of an impact, you ask? Well, after Bloombergville was shut down, many of those protesters decided to directly support the call made by the media foundation Adbusters to Occupy Wall Street on September 17. Bloombergville inspired an insatiable enthusiasm for the strategy, as well as what turned out to be an essential experience base facilitating "General Assemblies." General Assembly meetings are central to these occupations because they allow anyone to make his or her voice heard. This drives the movement, as it empowers people who would otherwise not participate. So Bloombergville laid the foundation for Occupy Wall Street in this and many other ways, and I don't believe the movement would have worked without this core of battle-tested early adopters.

These kinds of experiences convinced me that the movements stemming from Occupy Wall Street in New York and the uprising in Wisconsin have been one and the same. This was brought home to me in July when I went back to Wisconsin to help out during the state senate recalls, which were a direct result of the capitol occupation. Even amidst the recall excitement, some of the activists I admire most could not have been more emphatic in expressing their gratitude for the inspiration we helped provide from Bloombergville.

I also felt this same solidarity-fused sentiment while walking around #Occupy events in New York, especially when wearing the too-ridiculous-to-ignore cheeseheads. Such Wisconsin symbolism caused a constant barrage of comments like, "Hey, Wisconsin! You all started this. Thank you!" It was gratifying beyond belief to represent all of Wisconsin with the Job Party at Occupy Wall Street events, particularly since I could then pass along pictures and video of such sentiments to further inspire the folks back home.

So it goes with the reciprocal inspiration boomerang, and who knows whose psychological barrier will break tomorrow because of it! Yet even though the All-American Wisconsin occupation that we were able to follow up close and personal was the impetus for so many people to get active across the nation, this is all tied to something much bigger. For example, that same Skype session we held with Walkerville was directly preceded by one with a tent city in Barcelona.

Just as Wisconsin provided an essential foundation for Occupy Wall Street, so too did Spain. That's where the General Assembly process first originated, which they were able to pass on to us through social media. It was the same broader trend in Tunisia, Egypt, and every other social-media-powered movement across the globe. This viral boomerang effect is rapidly increasing the number of activists who can learn from and be inspired by each others' valiant fight on behalf of the 99 percent.

These Internet-powered occupations provide a whole new platform for citizens the world over to communicate and collaborate, obliterating psychological barriers in more and more of us in the process. I am a case in point. In less than six months I've gone from being unable to speak at that April meeting with the Egyptian protesters to helping organize an Occupy the Board Room rally for which an Egyptian youth protester flew from Cairo just to show us some "solidarity and support." This is so much bigger than politics alone. It demonstrates just how close and like-minded our global community really is. Through the power of social media, we are building inspiration-inducing relationships between revolutionaries of all kinds. The resulting impact on our society cannot be underestimated.

THE ACCIDENTAL ACTIVIST

Lisa Epstein

Lisa Epstein, founder of ForeclosureHamlet.org, is part of a small group of Floridians who continue to research and expose the foreclosure fraud scandal. A former nurse committed to social and economic justice for the millions of families across America, her belief is that only through education and community activism will we change a system that is so damaging to all but the financial institutions that continue to be unjustly enriched.

As a forty-four-year-old mother and nurse working in a Florida cancer clinic, I believed that I'd long ago found my calling, my way of making a difference in the lives of others. I was skilled at providing comfort, information, and support to families when they were confronted with a devastating, life-changing diagnosis. But aside from my calling, I was always an introvert, living an anonymous life. I never imagined I'd become an accidental activist, speaking out against fraudulent foreclosures as I try to help save families' homes and prevent the breakdown of communities caused by mass foreclosures.

It all began in early 2008, when my husband's business failed. Our marriage failed soon after. I had lived a frugal life, well under my means, paying bills on time and maintaining my high credit score. Determined to mitigate my reduced financial circumstances, I immediately started calling the bank to which I'd been paying my monthly mortgage payments in hopes of starting the process of a loan workout or any other sustainable option. I mistakenly believed eight months of adequate savings to cushion the loss of my husband's income would give me plenty of time to work out a long-term solution with the bank. As my savings dwindled month by month, I dealt with a bureaucratic nightmare and a maze of conflicting information and outright false promises. I depleted my savings to avoid falling behind in my payments. By the fall of 2008, I was advised by bank representatives to cease making payments for three to four months in order to qualify for assistance. I strongly resisted this advice but had no viable alternative. I felt sick and anxious the entire three months as I held back the monthly payments.

At the three-and-a-half-month mark, there was a knock at the door. It was a process server with the delivery of a foreclosure lawsuit, filed by a bank that was wholly unfamiliar to me. I was being sued by a bank with which I had no financial relationship. The bank attorneys presented claims and legal documents that to my untrained eye were patently fraudulent. It's clear to me now that their instruction to withhold payments for three months was simply one of the many routes on the road to a manufactured foreclosure.

And so it goes with millions of other stunned homeowners. But something drove me to resist. I was compelled to act, and I couldn't stop until I got to the bottom of a situation that I knew was horribly wrong.

It took me a few weeks to get my bearings. Then I started to research, to educate myself. I learned how a foreclosure is processed and how to access my county's property records. I studied the financial wizardry called "mortgage-backed securities" that Wall Street used to gamble with the homes, savings, and pensions of tens of millions of Americans. I read about the dangers of repealing financial legislation like the Glass-Steagall law, which was put in place after the Great Depression, and the Commodities Futures Modernization Act, which allowed staggering bets upon bets of these complex fraud investments. During my lunch break, I would take the twelve-minute walk to the courthouse (a seven-minute run if I was short of time) and observe foreclosure court proceedings or read foreclosure files. I found widespread evidence of fraudulent documents.

The more I dug, the more I realized this mess came about long before countless families obligated themselves to predatory, unsustainable mortgages. Predatory financial institutions were already hell bent on gambling with American families' homes. A complex "financial innovation" enabled bait-and-switch mortgages and promissory notes to be bundled by the thousands and repackaged over and over. This garbage was somehow magically transformed into falsely rated so-called "safe" investments and sold back to the investing public while profiteering middlemen were rewarded with huge bonuses. It was the financial services industry, not the American families facing foreclosure, that diabolically spent decades and hundreds of millions of lobbying dollars repealing Depression-era banking regulations. Then, during America's home lending boom from 2003 to 2007, the mortgage lenders and Wall Street banks ignored or willfully violated basic fundamentals of safe loan processing as well as statutory, legal, and contractual procedures for authentic real estate conveyance.

This crash course on fiscal malfeasance transformed me into an outspoken agitator dedicated to both exposing the fraud that lies behind America's foreclosure crisis and supporting those affected. It is immoral and unethical for the leaders of a country to allow our citizens to be dispossessed. But the situation was even more abhorrent: I realized that almost every foreclosure and eviction was based on the most massive financial fraud in history, a financial fraud that continues to this day.

Now, deep in a prolonged recession, with so many people unable to meet extortionate home loan payment terms, it has come to light that the banks and their foreclosure mills have fabricated many millions of fraudulent documents to prove the unknown—that is, which bank legally owns which mortgages. To this day, many citizens, the media, and a seeming majority of politicians have bought into the banks' propaganda that irresponsible American homeowners are the root cause of the financial crisis and therefore should rightly bear the full responsibility, shame, and stigma of their own personal foreclosure misfortunes.

But I know a predator when I see one. After spending two decades as an oncology nurse, working with both adults and children diagnosed with cancer, I quickly recognized the predatory behavior of the financial sector's foreclosure enterprise, which is deeply implicated in the global financial crisis. Cancer is the uncontrolled growth of abnormal cells in the body, cells that refuse to honor boundaries and that usurp all available resources to the grave danger of the host. The foreclosure enterprise was so familiar to me, consisting of savage predators stalking and ambushing prey, indiscriminately extracting their victims' critical resources while remaining disdainful of boundaries, encroaching on once healthy productive families and leaving them destitute, dispossessed, evicted, and homeless.

For almost twenty years, I watched my patients and their families cope with the financial struggles that come with a devastating medical diagnosis and observed how they worked out solutions with their mortgage lenders. But in 2007, something changed. Families were unable to negotiate the gauntlet of mortgage debt collectors. I started to hear my patients' real fears over impending foreclosure lawsuits. Then foreclosure happened to me, marking the point where my world became wholly unrecognizable.

I am far from alone in my outrage and determination. I am part of a small group of anti-foreclosure fraud activists who have put everything we have into breaking the story of widespread foreclosure fraud. Building on the work of the earliest foreclosure fraud experts, Nye Lavalle, April Charney, and Max Gardner, the six of

us—Michael Redman (founder of 4closureFraud.org), Florida lawyers Lynn Szymoniak, Matt Weidner, and Thomas Ice of Ice Legal,
along with Thomas's wife Ariane and I—were driven by an un-
shakable confidence that once the story broke detailing widespread
criminal activity surrounding fraudulent foreclosure practices, an
immediate moratorium would be imposed. We anticipated there
would be reasoned solutions that would help keep families in their
homes. We were sure that there would be a halt to the massive
nationwide dispossessions, evictions, and depletion of retirement
fund savings. We confidently expected speedy investigations, prosecutions, and indictments of the financiers who knowingly implemented the heinous scheme that impoverished tens of millions of
Americans through fraudulent home loans and investments sold
under the guise of safe investments for our municipalities, retirement savings, and college funds.

We were wrong. There have been few investigations and no
prosecutions or indictments of the very financial services elites who
have brought our country to its knees. Instead, there remained so
much more work, education, and fraud exposure to be done.

It turned out that, like me, many families, attorneys, judges,
regulators, legislators, law enforcers, local recorders of land ownership documents, reporters, and citizens were completely unin-
formed about the history of the financial crisis and the resulting
foreclosures. So I started to build a network of professionals and
community members and held monthly "Foreclosure Fraud Happy
Hours"[34] to discuss the foreclosure crisis and foreclosure fraud. I
faxed and e-mailed and leafleted invitations to foreclosure defense
attorneys, community organizations, and news media.

To encourage families facing foreclosure to shed the cloak of
shame and fear, and to share stories, information, and experiences,
in 2008 I created a blog—ForeclosureHamlet.org. I chose *Hamlet*
for its double meaning, a Shakespearean tragedy and a small town.
The Web site has over four thousand members and receives approximately three thousand hits per day. I have written e-mails and

papers and read, studied, and held poorly attended protests. For months, I tried to promote weekly "Moratorium Monday" protests outside my county courthouse where tens of thousands of foreclosure cases have been filed since the housing bust and are dispensed in thirty-second hearings. I allowed myself three hours of sleep a night. I repeatedly contacted elected officials and members of law enforcement.

I find that so many of my nursing skills are enormously valuable in my activism work. Being a nurse is to be highly precise balanced with a great deal of empathy for families in distress. Nurses are oftentimes tasked with conveying new and complex information to frightened and wounded people. Nurses also encourage families to develop coping mechanisms and to channel grief and fear in a nondestructive manner. The same skills that enable me to work effectively with patients and with families facing fraudulent foreclosures are also necessary when working with foreclosure fraud defense attorneys. I find that many attorneys who take up the cause of foreclosure fraud defense work do so not only to help their clients avoid an illegal foreclosure and eviction but also because they are desperate to preserve the fading integrity of our judicial system. Each week I field calls from stunned, shocked, and mourning attorneys who have witnessed the complete breakdown of the rule of law. Their grief mirrors my own.

When the Florida Supreme Court appointed a task force on residential foreclosures, I submitted comments in an attempt to educate the court about the widespread fabrication of documents and fraud upon Florida courts by banks and their foreclosure mill law firms.[35] The Florida Supreme Court ordered the verification of all foreclosure lawsuits against much opposition from banks and their lawyers. Florida was the first state to impose such a requirement. I, along with others, shared foreclosure fraud and property document fraud information with the New Jersey judiciary and the Hawaii legislature. Now those two states, in addition to New York, Kentucky, Ohio, Massachusetts, and Nevada, have passed laws or procedures that attempt to reduce fraudulent foreclosures.[36]

I also advised people to attend foreclosure court proceedings to bear witness to a process that allows innocent families to lose their homes in fraudulent foreclosures with the stamp of approval of Florida's elected judges. Typical of reports that came in from across the state of Florida was this one: "We are not allowed in the courtrooms to observe foreclosure proceedings." Seemingly insurmountable obstacles have been purposefully placed by the banks and judicial system each step of the way: from deciphering the impenetrable legalese that enshrouds the documents, to attempting to determine the proper foreclosing entity, to examining the validity of previously unassailable documents such as affidavits and assignments of mortgage, to navigating the unfamiliar territory common to all legal proceedings.

After I informed first amendment lawyers, the ACLU, and other constitutional scholars of multiple reports of exclusionary policies in Florida's courts, letters by these individuals and organizations were volleyed back and forth with Florida Supreme Court Justice Charles Canady, who finally wrote to all Florida courts that "the chief judges shall ensure that the judges they supervise and the staff who report to those judges, as well as bailiffs and employees of the clerks of court, are not violating the rights of Floridians by improperly closing judicial proceedings to the public."[37] A year after Justice Canady wrote that directive, I still receive e-mails from people who continue to be refused entry into Florida courtrooms where foreclosure proceedings are taking place.

My activism has come at much personal cost. The stress has been so intense that most of my hair fell out. I lost my job. I've often doubted and questioned myself. One night, Rosa Parks, the famous civil rights activist, came to me in a dream. She sat on the side of my bed, reached out for my hand, and simply held it for many minutes. She looked at me and nodded. And then she faded into mist. It was just the inspiration I needed to keep going.

After that dream, I started working in earnest, nonstop. I spent full days at the courthouse. I talked to hundreds and then thousands of families. In order to do this work, I have made many sacrifices, but the toughest has been giving up time with my four-year-old daughter. For three years now, I have been unable to be silent or live my quiet former life, and my little girl has had to share my focus and attention with the millions of dispossessed people I am fighting for. I am deeply appreciative of my good friend Mary Delaguila who, as a loving second mother to my daughter, has enabled me to spend time at the courthouse and at events and meetings, as well as researching and writing reports.

And I don't know if my daughter will get all the attention she deserves from her mother any time soon, because my mission is far from complete. To this day, most judges refuse to acknowledge any bank fraud or misconduct, instead revealing their unyielding bank bias by ruling to throw families out of their homes instead of scrutinizing and questioning highly suspect documents produced by the bank and their lawyers. Florida's Fourth District Court of Appeal is bank-friendly to the point where judges reverse their own court opinions at the urging of lawyers representing the banks. Banks continue to break laws, abuse their customers, and prey upon American families.[38]

Each year, Florida's lawmakers introduce and vote on legislation to speed up foreclosures by reducing both procedures and oversight those banks should—but don't—currently follow. In 2010, we arranged a set of buses to travel up to Tallahassee to oppose the first of these bills. We used imagery from the civil rights Freedom Rides, hiring buses to travel across the state overnight for a day of demonstrations at Florida's capitol. We repeated this trek in 2011. We are gearing up to go again in 2012. Each year, these bills get closer and closer to passage.

Since I began this activism, the entire conversation has changed. Because of this unprecedented fraud, a new lexicon has emerged, now adopted by legislators, judges, and the mainstream media;

words like *robosigning, foreclosure mills*, and *fraudclosure* are terms
that Americans have become familiar with. Profound issues such as
document and notary fraud have made national headlines. Across
the country, county recorders of deeds have spoken out, outraged
that the banks' fraud has defiled our nation's property records,
muddying property ownership and legal boundaries, not to mention the hundreds of millions of dollars lost to local governments
due to a massive evasion of recording fees. Three foreclosure mills
have gone down in flames[39] and many others are under investigation or have signed settlement agreements. The State of Nevada has
recently sued Lender Processing Services (LPS), an integral hub
of the foreclosure fraud network, detailing an incestuous relationship between banks, foreclosure lawyers, and LPS. There are ongoing consent orders between federal banking regulators—Office of
the Comptroller of the Currency, the FDIC, the Office of Thrift
Supervision, the Federal Reserve—and fourteen of the nation's
biggest financial institutions.[40] State attorneys general in New
York, Nevada, and Delaware have come out with very strong investigations or lawsuits. In addition, Massachusetts attorney general
Martha Coakley announced the first major lawsuit against Bank of
America, JP Morgan Chase, Citigroup, Wells Fargo, GMAC/Ally,
as well as Mortgage Electronic Registration Systems (MERS) and
its parent MERSCorp—some of the biggest names in the foreclosure enterprise.

Several states have passed legislation to protect their citizens,
constitutional due process, and constitutional property rights. More
judges are educated on this issue and are publishing decisions holding banks to the same laws to which the rest of us are held. Nevada
has criminalized foreclosure fraud, and immediately upon the law
becoming effective, foreclosures essentially ceased in that state. One
federal government agency, the Federal Housing Finance Agency,
sued eighteen banks for loan origination, underwriting, and securities fraud. Another federal agency, the Department of Housing
and Urban Development, sued Deutsche Bank for origination and

underwriting fraud. Many state and county agencies are suing the fraudulent mortgage database company MERS.

As part of the banking regulators' consent orders with the financial institutions implicated in commission of foreclosure fraud, the Office of the Comptroller of the Currency has generously allowed the banks themselves to hire friendly, industry insider "independent" reviewers to scrutinize 4.5 million foreclosures that were initiated between 2009 and 2010 for harm done to families. Of course, this ignores the millions of fraudulent foreclosure actions that occurred outside of this two-year period. For those foreclosures which fit into the narrow time frame, reports from inquisitive and insightful reporters are emerging that question the validity of this process and cast doubt on the possibility of any meaningful relief for families who have fraudulently lost their homes.[41] The New York Banking Supervisor has settlement orders with five mortgage servicers demanding all in-process fraud-tainted foreclosures be dismissed from the New York courts.[42]

However, there have been huge disappointments along with these incremental victories. A fifty-state attorneys general foreclosure fraud investigative panel was formed in the fall of 2010. We had much hope in this multi-state panel, but it too has succumbed to bank interests and has since been disgraced. More than one attorney general has been publicly chastised for taking campaign contributions from foreclosure fraud–related companies that are currently targets of investigations.[43] The panel did propose a very weak settlement, offering complete immunity, no admissions of guilt or wrongdoing, and, worse, no meaningful investigation.

The progress we've made has been greatly muted by ongoing revelations of gross corruption. For example, in March of 2011 the Law Offices of Marshall C. Watson paid a $2 million settlement with the state for foreclosure fraud-related activities. Following the signing of the settlement, it came to light that the Watson firm had cultivated a relationship with then-director of the economic crimes unit at the Office of the Florida Attorney General, Mary

Leontakianakos, who allowed the original $7 million settlement to be watered down to the final sum of $2 million. Shortly thereafter, Ms. Leontakianakos left the Florida attorney general's office to work at the Watson firm.[44] Then it came to light that Broward County, Florida, Chief Judge Victor Tobin, who presided over foreclosure fraud cases and was instrumental in setting court foreclosure policies, had been secretly negotiating with the Watson firm for employment, which began the day after he quit the bench.

One of the most frightening aspects of the foreclosure fraud crisis is the ugly realization that the financial sector has corrupted, on both federal and state levels, our three branches of government, law enforcement, and regulatory agencies. Most people in public office ignored or dismissed us, but we found a few public servants and investigative reporters willing to listen to and review our findings. Two assistant attorneys general in the Florida attorney general's office quickly grasped the enormity of the scheme. June Clarkson and Theresa Edwards were the first government attorneys to investigate foreclosure mills and document fabrication shops and other foreclosure enterprise corporations, such as LPS and Nationwide Title Clearing. These two women released information and updates on their investigations during the last six months of Bill McCollum's tenure as Florida attorney general. Unfortunately, his successor, Pam Bondi, publicly declared her disdain for Florida's families subjected to fraudulent foreclosures, denied the findings of her own office, and implemented a policy of cooperation with the targets of the investigation. Shortly after Bondi's administration took over, Clarkson and Edwards were fired from their jobs without reason or warning.[45] After Clarkson and Edwards were unceremoniously ousted, it became public that Bondi had accepted dozens of campaign contributions from the very targets of her office's investigation. This story, a clear example of corruption of elected officials by harmful financial institutions, continues to capture national attention.

Fraudulent foreclosures have been allowed to continue, blessed by judges, lawmakers, and law enforcement. Three hundred years of property ownership records, started back in colonial times, have been completely adulterated. Untold numbers of elderly people, children, people with disabilities, veterans, active-duty deployed military service members, young families, and long-established community members across the economic strata have faced foreclosures and evictions, and many have had their entire life savings depleted. I imagine if these atrocities were happening in another country, the United States would intervene, perhaps with military force, to bring aid to those people and to pressure their government to cease wrongful actions against their own citizens.

But it is happening here, in America, and there has been no meaningful governmental intervention.

More and more citizens are becoming educated. Journalists and financial writers are gaining knowledge and writing articles that continue to expose the truth behind the millions of fraudulent foreclosures. Anti-eviction protesters and local Occupy Wall Street groups are demonstrating against and opposing foreclosures and evictions, articulating moral outrage now that widespread foreclosure fraud continues to be exposed. In October 2011, I became active in launching our own OWS movement in Palm Beach, and I often stop by the campsite to talk to its main participants, although their numbers are dwindling. I am involved in the fledgling national Occupy Our Homes group, which is focused purely on the housing crisis and is organizing anti-foreclosure, anti-eviction, and housing rights actions on a national level.

A year after the foreclosure fraud story started breaking in the mainstream media, the foreclosures continue. Governmental attempts to investigate have been greatly weakened by political interests. Outside of Nevada's attorney general Catherine Masto's criminal complaint filed in November 2011 against fraudulent document fabricators, prosecutions are completely nonexistent. A few courageous elected officials, mostly on the county or state level, are speaking out and fighting for the rule of law, for justice. They number fewer than ten.

My own personal fight continues, alongside my activism. Up to now, although the property remains in litigation, I've managed to keep the marital residence, which is my daughter's home when she is with her father. I often consider dropping back into an anonymous life, quietly working at some service industry job and raising my daughter. But in the end, two things compel me to continue my work: the families who have been affected and my horror at our system that continues to allow mass dispossession based on fraud. I've met or corresponded with thousands of people struggling in a bank-generated economic crisis, desperate to keep their homes: young people and the elderly, the unemployed and those with disabilities, the veterans and the young families, the single people, and those with no alternative housing options. The hopelessness and grief, fear, and terror are palpable. These dire circumstances have even triggered murders and suicides, and no doubt the extreme stress has brought countless homeowners to a state of ill health or an early demise. There is no recourse against property fraud, bank home invasions, fraudulent evictions, or foreclosure fraud in most courts across America, and those in power are complicit by allowing these acts to continue.

History and hindsight will not be kind when archiving these events. At the very least, let the record reflect that a few of us who understood the scheme stood up and spoke out and refused to be silenced.

Our work continues.

MY TRAJECTORY WITH OCCUPY

Suresh Naidu

Suresh Naidu is assistant professor of economics and public affairs at Columbia University. He spends a lot of time thinking about economic history and the political economy of development.

There had been small flutters about an upcoming demonstration on Wall Street through the occasional mention on mailing lists that I mostly ignore. I assumed it would be like so many other actions I've been to in my life, where a small group of the usual suspects in the activist community showed up, tried to make a small ruckus, and went home, or the protest got broken up by the police. That said, I was still intrigued by the idea of mounting an occupation, even if temporary, in the heart of the financial district, which even many professional economists hold accountable for much of the inefficiency and inequality of recent years.

So when it began on September 17, I called an old anarchist friend of mine and asked, "Are you going to this thing?" He said no, and, since he was much more connected to activist circles than I was, I assumed it wasn't going to be all that momentous. I stayed in my office doing research while watching the occupation unfold on live stream, and it seemed benign enough. I was glad that "the kids" were still fighting the good fight despite how futile it looked. I also remember deliberating about how it would be perceived by my more senior economist colleagues at Columbia if I publicly supported such a fringe event, and I chose to not endorse the movement on Facebook. As political scientist Corey Robin writes, fear induced by the workplace is as potent a silencer as anything else.

And yet the tenacity of the occupation surprised me, and another friend and I decided to schedule a hangout at the occupation to give our support. So the next night, a Friday, we spent at Zuccotti Park in the pouring rain. Since I didn't recognize anybody in the General Assembly, we hung around for a bit, ate a leisurely dinner from one of the nearby halal trucks, and left. That was my first experience of the occupation: wet, rainy and dark, with a General Assembly of about fifteen to twenty people, and a Styrofoam container of spicy chicken-over-rice. I was supportive but not completely optimistic.

In two days, however, all that changed when New York police officer Anthony Bologna pepper sprayed two women who were kettled in that now infamous video. The following Friday, my wife and I went to a solidarity march at Police Plaza. Afterwards, I posted on Facebook that this march had more anger and energy than anything I'd seen in the United States since the anti-globalization movement of 1999 to 2001, in which I had been heavily involved as a university student. Once my wife left for the Middle East, I threw myself into Occupy Wall Street with full abandon. From then on, it was an intense few weeks of rallies and actions that tore my fall plans of submitting research papers to shreds. Finally, after many years, I again felt that mildly addictive chemical kick of successful collective action.

I'm an economist down to my bones, so I can't turn off the part of my brain that is constantly spinning mathematical models and thinking of ways of measuring the things I'm interested in. So I wrote a blog post that became somewhat popular on interpreting OWS through the lens of formal models of democratization. Also, in response to the somewhat ridiculous slogans about money and finance being bandied around Zuccotti Park, an economist friend of mine from the Center for Popular Economics and I began doing economics teach-ins on Sunday mornings. We discussed the politics of monetary policy, how the banking system works, and what alternative economic institutions would look like. Attendance was high, the reception was really positive, and these teach-ins were some of the most rewarding activities I did during the occupation.

To quote a friend, the movement was "leaderful" as much as it was "leaderless," with particular people playing decisive roles in particular working groups for short periods but no individual or group having a full picture or any sense of control overall of the activities going on. The organization of park logistics was a kind of communist invisible hand where, despite the lack of centralized decision making, things that needed to get done were getting done. People were cooperating and making things happen without prices and without centralized planning!

This organic process of self-organization got my social science antenna wobbling attentively as it seemed to repudiate both Hayek and Keynes at the same time. (Hayek argued that markets and prices were the best way to communicate local information about what was needed and how to provide it; Keynes thought that coordination on a larger scale was necessary to get resources to their best uses.) Instead, Zuccotti Park's organization was both decentralized and non-market, an ideal of anarchist principles that I had generally come across only in my research on hunter-gatherer populations.

Nevertheless, it was clear that the General Assembly, while empowering in a congregationalist way, was quickly becoming unwieldy for the kinds of logistical decisions that needed to get made (e.g., long-run budgeting). A model of decision making we had used in the anti-globalization movement was the *spokescouncil*, which was a way to efficiently make large collective decisions and allocate speaking bandwidth without sacrificing direct democracy and decentralization. Based on my experience with the spokescouncil in 1999 and 2001, I jumped into the working group handling structure, and from there I learned a lot about the inner workings of OWS. I briefly wandered into the finance working group as well, helped out with a few tasks there, and then retreated into helping craft the proposal to form a spokescouncil.

That wound up taking a lot of time, and it turned into an experience I had been trying to avoid: presenting and passing a proposal through the General Assembly. Long story short: after three hours, during which my more informed co–working group members did most of the talking, our proposal was blocked and tabled. So we promised to hold daily teach-ins about how the spokescouncil would work, and every day for much of the next week I was in Zuccotti Park. But, lo and behold, a week later it was passed! Spokescouncil was born. In the interests of full disclosure, it was by no means an immediate success, and I was certainly despairing about OWS group dynamics the weekend before the eviction.

But the story is by no means over. I was there during the night of the eviction and during the actions on November 17, and my optimism has not really been blunted despite the loss of the park. Maybe it should have been, but today there's a plan to do what I call "direct action balance sheet relief" and occupy and defend a foreclosed property in Brooklyn. As we go to press, there is a meeting scheduled during which OWS quantitative-trading dissidents will be drafting public comments on the Volcker Rule in the Dodd-Frank bill on financial reform. There is a lot more to talk about, including how OWS has changed what I can discuss with my colleagues and students, and the network of amazing activist colleagues it has reconstructed. I'm still an economic historian; I don't think we will know whether OWS has had an impact or not for at least a decade. So for now, I'm taking the plunge, taking to the streets, and hoping that others do the same. Let's see what happens.

DAVID IPPOLITO:
OCCUPY WALL STREET'S WOODY GUTHRIE

David Ippolito is an American singer, songwriter, and playwright who lives in New York City. He has self-released eight albums and is best known for his weekly summer performances in Central Park, which have been attended by thousands of people. He styles himself as "That Guitar Man from Central Park." Ippolito also performs at venues throughout New York City, including an annual December performance at Merkin Concert Hall as well as year-round shows at the Leonard Nimoy Thalia–Symphony Space, The Red Lion on Bleecker Street, and Jim Caruso's Cast Party, held at the famous Birdland Music Club.

He recently wrote this song about the greed and corruption of our financial and political system, which became something of a folk anthem for the Occupy Wall Street crowd. It is a rewrite of his song "Where'dat Money Go?" from his 2004 album Common Ground. *A video of the song can be found at www.youtube.com/watch?v=7annSXf7uDo.*

THE OCCUPY WALL STREET RAG

We all watched Wall Street and the banks bailed out without a fight
'Cause our store-bought politicians rigged the game.
And we say just cuz you say it's legal . . . that don't make it right.
We're here . . . and Occupy Wall Street is our name.
And we're gonna crank the volume now. We're turnin' up the heat.
Fair-minded people everywhere are takin' it to the street.

[CHORUS]
  Singin'—Where is the honesty? Where's the integrity?
  Where's the love? And where'dat money go?
  It's clear the people wanna see a little accountability.
  Where's the love? And where'dat money go?

We've never seen the gap between the rich and poor so wide.
And good hard-workin' people wonder why.
But the deck was stacked, and that's a fact that cannot be denied
By the very best government money can buy.
Some right-wing pundits sneer that we're just shiftless malcontents,
But that narrow view is missin' who this movement represents.

Say . . . We the 99 percent demand of this establishment
Where's the love? And where'dat money go?
Now's the time to stand up proud. Let me hear you sing it loud.
Where's the love? And where'dat money go?

Well, it's not just New York City now. We've grown from town to town.
All around the world the feelin's everywhere

And we'll sing out louder every time they try to shut us down
So in the end they can't pretend that we're not there.
And they're about to see how peacefully we express a little
   rage
And we'll vote 'em out, cuz we could do without a second
   "Gilded Age."

We're the 99 percent, hand-in-hand and confident.
Where's the love? And where' dat money go?
It's time for you to stand up proud. Let me hear you sing it
   loud.
Where's the love? And where' dat money go?

Where is the honesty? Where's the integrity?
Where's the love? And where' dat money go?
We're the 99 percent, hand-in-hand and confident.
Where's the love? And where' dat money go?
Where's the love?

(SHOUT) And where' dat money go!?

OCCUPY LONDON

OVERVIEW

Much like the United States, the United Kingdom emerged from the maelstrom of the financial crisis battered and bleeding. The bursting of the bank-fueled bubble had exposed many a festering long-term problem. The economy was shakier than anyone had admitted. Demand was feeble. As in the United States, debt-financed consumption had papered over underlying weaknesses. Investments in infrastructure, especially industrial infrastructure, had been inadequate for years, and now it was showing.

There were many serious problems with the British economy, and the most serious one was the weak demand. So it was interesting when the government of Prime Minister David Cameron made deficit reduction the pillar of its recovery plan.

As in the United States, the United Kingdom had run up a deficit in times of economic growth. That left government finances in a somewhat precarious position at the time of the crisis, when there was really an economic imperative for spending, even if it meant an increase in the deficit. Following bank bailouts that seemed critical to keeping the economy from completely collapsing—even if they did not seem particularly just—Britain found itself in 2009 with a deficit that had grown to more than 11 percent of its GDP. It was the largest deficit the country had run since World War II.

This, clearly, was going to become a problem. However, considering the growing numbers of out-of-work Britons, failing businesses, and increasing hardship for regular people, it was hard to argue it was the most urgent one. But the government did anyway. To deal with the dual problems of a ballooning deficit and a struggling economy, they had two basic paths to choose from. On the one hand, they could try to improve growth with a targeted boost in government spending on the neglected infrastructure and other measures that would put people back to work. This would increase economic activity, which in turn would improve tax receipts, which in turn would improve the fiscal position. Or they could simply cut expenditures—in other words, cut the public services and social safety nets that more people were depending on in this time of need.

They chose the latter, and it seemed almost like the panicked response of someone who pours water on a grease fire. True, the immediate deficit-to-GDP ratio would be reduced. But the damage to the economy—it was not hard to see that unemployment would grow and most people's spending power decrease—would eventually do equal or greater damage to GDP. Of course, when both the numerator and denominator of a fraction decrease, the result is a number of a similar size. Austerity would not greatly improve the long-term deficit-to-GDP ratio. Much worse still, the policy would inflict additional unnecessary suffering on workers.

There was, however, another dimension to the government's set of fiscal and economic policies, which made it seem less like a panicked response and maybe a bit more nefarious. For one thing, not everyone was doing badly. The banks that had been bailed out were once again bonus-happy. With ultralow interest rates, they could afford it. Meanwhile, the long-term political agenda of the right was being accomplished under the guise of urgent economic necessity.

Whether or not it was a deliberate plan, it added up to this: a shift toward a society in which the middle class and poor were left behind. Taxpayers subsidized big corporations, especially banks, and saved them when they failed, and deregulation paved the way for ever-increasing inequality.

There was gathering unease and anger. And when Occupy Wall Street kicked off in the United States, it made these feelings fully formed and actionable. It was time for outright protest. Activists now had the critical mass to mobilize and a model on which to base their movement—and even improve on the occupation concept pioneered in New York. Thus, in mid-October 2011, Occupy London was born with an initial encampment set up in front of St. Paul's Cathedral in the heart of London's financial district.

At press time, the movement was fighting legal actions attempting dispersal, and as with their American counterparts, the next move was not crystal clear. One thing, at least, was plain: no longer would it be taken for granted in the United Kingdom that the path to economic redemption meant austerity and sacrifice from people who did not make the mess.

THE OCCUPIED TIMES

Martin Eirmann and Steven Maclean

Martin Eiermann is a German journalist and managing editor of the political magazine The European *and of the* Occupied Times.

Steven Maclean is a freelance journalist, Huffington Post *blogger, activist, world traveler, and the executive editor of the* Occupied Times.

On October 15, activists in London rallied at St. Paul's Cathedral to occupy the adjacent Paternoster Square, home of the London Stock Exchange and center of the so-called "Square Mile," the heart of London's financial district. When police blocked access to the square and the private owner revoked access rights, a camp was established around St. Paul's Cathedral and quickly grew to over two hundred tents. Eviction seemed likely several times. After key figures within the church resigned from their posts in protest, the Anglican Church reversed course. Occupy London was allowed to stay. Even the City of London—a private entity posing as a publicly elected local government—withdrew its first eviction notice (but has since resumed legal action). Five weeks in, Occupy London had two camps, three occupied sites, several kitchens, a piano tent, a university, welfare counseling, a weekend kindergarten, and a newspaper. This is a brief history of that paper, the *Occupied Times.*

Let's begin with two assertions to frame the story: The moment that a movement becomes newsworthy, it begins to lose control over its narrative. And the more it grows, the harder it is to sustain a genuine exchange of ideas within the movement and among its constituent individuals. There is nothing wrong with losing control. It would be preposterous for anyone to claim that a single, coherent, controlled narrative had to emerge from a movement as diverse and fluid as the occupy movement. We tend to welcome the diversity of views and interests—after all, it is the perceived lack of creative dissidence and political imagination that brought many of us to the camp at St. Paul's in the first place.

Yet within a week of the occupation of St. Paul's Cathedral in London, it felt like public opinion was shaped not by people's personal impressions at the camp (or by actions at the camp), but by what the *Guardian* or the *Evening Standard* would report, which, even if well intentioned, was selective at best. At the same time, the expanding infrastructure of the growing occupy camp in London meant that more people would need to spend more time in working group discussions and maintenance work, and that critical discussions would often happen outside of the twice-daily General Assemblies.

The idea for the *Occupied Times* was born out of these concerns (and, to give proper credit, from the example set by the *Occupied Wall Street Journal* in New York). On October 19, four days after the start of the occupation at St. Paul's, my colleague and coauthor of this piece, Steve Maclean, went to work. Within four days, the newspaper went from nonexistence to a core staff of almost a dozen; a fully equipped newsroom tent with whiteboards, news desks, a contact database; and a shaky Internet connection. Within five days, we had gathered enough content to fill the inaugural edition and secured a local printer that agreed to help us out with a print run of two thousand copies. We had a team of news reporters, editors, copy editors (many of them with professional journalism experience), a photographer, two layout experts who were willing to work night shifts, and an ever-expanding cast of willing contributors from inside and outside the camp. Some of us stayed at the St. Paul's camp, and some did not. On October 26, less than a week after our first meeting, issue #1 of the *Occupied Times* rolled off the printing presses.

It is easy to gloss over the initial challenges with the benefit of hindsight. When we first gathered, we had little but a healthy dose of optimism and a willingness to improvise. No Internet? There's always a Starbucks nearby. No whiteboards? Maybe someone can trade with the tech team. When there is a will, there is most likely a way as well.

While none of us had ever attempted to launch a newspaper from scratch before, our collective journalism expertise proved invaluable. Even in the first meeting, much of the discussion focused on the very real decisions involved in setting up a sustainable publication routine. Would we have a separate editorial department? What journalistic code of conduct did we envision for ourselves? What criteria would we use to select and edit articles? And what layout did we envision for the paper? If anything, we tended to over-engineer the project before being dragged back into pragmatic improvisation. Yet many of these early discussions never ended— we are still meeting to discuss our vision for the paper and its role within the occupy movement. We are still trying to approach each edition with a fresh perspective, and trying to make it better than the previous one. So this might be an appropriate place to pause and reflect on a few fundamental questions: What is the *Occupied Times*? What is it trying to do, and how is it trying to achieve it? Even that question might be contested. *Should* we aspire to implement a long-term program within a movement that has preserved its fluidity and versatility? And from where do we derive the authority with which we now write editorials?

Indeed, many questions about the newspaper cannot be answered conclusively by us. The paper is very much the product of our shared desires and ambitions. If they change, the paper will morph accordingly. New contributors introduce new ideas as well, and we must not be hesitant in embracing them. The only thing we can do here is share our thoughts.

The paper, we decided, would be published weekly, a schedule that gives us sufficient time to organize twelve newspaper-sized pages of content once the previous edition has been sent to the printer and still supplies the camps with a steady flow of coverage. The print edition would focus on in-depth news analysis, opinion pieces, and longer features. Breaking news would often be published on our Web site or disseminated over Twitter. The idea was that the newspaper would complement rather than replace existing channels of communication and face-to-face discussions. It would be a forum for the exchange of ideas, rather than an official channel or an authoritative indicator of sentiments within the camps. It would be an educational opportunity for issues that have thus far ranged from fractional reserve banking to Christian theology and recycling. And, finally, it would be a paper that maintained a physical presence at the St. Paul's and Finsbury Square camps but aimed to transcend the confines of the occupied space by bringing in outside voices, addressing outside readers, and not shying away from confronting big issues head-on.

What does that mean in practice? We have tried to strike a balance between featuring articles on the camp—How is it organized? How does the consensus process work? Who runs the kitchen, and how can the camp liaison with local businesses and the church?—and articles that reflect ongoing discussions about the economy, politics, the need for reform, and the "media myths" that surround the occupy movement. Our reporters have spent many hours with the "night watch" team to report on their work. They have attended city meetings, profiled a homeless occupier, and spoken with camp counselors about mental health and women's safety issues. Three pages in each newspaper are devoted to local news and news analysis, and two additional pages are filled with news and features about other occupy camps or resistance movements elsewhere. Each newspaper also includes a debate section, where a hot topic is addressed in two opposing articles, one pro and one contra, as well as space for poems and cartoons. Two pages are devoted to economic coverage, and the centerfold features one or two longer stories about specific issues (such as the history of protest camps or the impact of the occupy movement on mainstream media discourses). There was even one feature that gave a voice to the bankers and analysts who work at the London Stock Exchange and passed through the camp before and after work.

Yet clearly the paper is not a substitute for being at the camp. Indeed, it was a conscious choice not to publish minutes from the daily General Assemblies. Partially that is due to our weekly publication schedule. There are better ways to disseminate that information, online via Twitter and offline on the notice boards throughout the camp. But we also felt that the newspaper needed to be conscious of its proper role within the larger camp. Logistics, organizational questions, procedural clarifications, and feedback for or from working groups are the stuff that keeps the camp going and makes it thrive. These discussions need to happen at the camp, among people, and in person. While it would be bizarre if the coverage in the paper did not reflect the general concerns and interests of the camp, it would be misleading to see the paper as a printed record of camp life.

Indeed, we are fully aware that a single paper cannot do justice to the variety of opinions within the camp. It was thus our intention to provide an alternative journalistic narrative and offer a platform for discussion. Against the narrowing scope of political discourse, we wanted to pit an army of daring ideas. Against the notion of inevitability, we wanted to raise challenges of creativity. And amidst the mainstream discourse, we wanted to shine light on paths less traveled. We hoped that campers at the London occupations would learn as much from our articles as did the visitors who stopped to pick up a copy.

The *Occupied Times* is thus a hybrid project: it is a newspaper written by campers for a larger audience, featuring articles that give voice to the range of opinions within the occupy movement. Yet it is also a newspaper for the camp, with features on camp life, portraits of individual occupiers, event listings from Tent City University (the educational hub of the London occupy movement), and a weekly debate section.

All of this means that we have to straddle many borders. We must reconcile the need for open debate with the constraints of our weekly publication schedule. In relation to the many issues discussed—sometimes very passionately—in the camp, we want to avoid taking sides. Our shared questions and individual convictions outnumber the conclusive answers we can give. And in relation to the mainstream media, we want to preserve our independence. We welcome outside voices and attention, but we must not become part of someone else's agenda.

Above all else, we want the *Occupied Times* to be a good newspaper. From the beginning, we set high editorial standards for ourselves. For each article, we ask ourselves a question: Would we be willing to defend the publication of this particular piece, even if we disagreed with its premise or viewpoint? We fact-check, we distinguish between statements of fact and personal opinion, and we pay attention to argumentative structures and language. Usually, we work with each contributor through one or more rounds of editing to make the articles as interesting and readable as possible. We want to be read not because of the paper's name but because of the quality of our content.

We are extremely fortunate to be working with two incredible designers, Lazaros and Tzortzis, who managed to distill all these ideas into a visual template for the paper. Their impossible task was to create something that was radical enough to mark the *Occupied Times* as a protest paper and advanced enough to avoid the trap of being dismissed by outside readers and becoming a self-referential and self-absorbed publication by activists, for activists. We settled for a combination of bold typography, large photographs, a readable text font, and a back cover that does double-duty as a demonstration placard. Like the rest of the newspaper, the design is always evolving, but we are starting from a very high baseline.

And, just like most things at the camp, this paper would not exist without the initiative, personal commitment, and helping hands of many. Countless campers have written for the *Occupied Times* or have helped with a myriad of other tasks, from setting up our newsroom tent to the folding and distribution of the printed papers. Steve, in particular, has sacrificed more than a few grey hairs and nights of sleep to build momentum and keep the paper running.

As we write this, the fifth edition is being shipped to the printer. The *Occupied Times* is now a familiar sight around St. Paul's every Wednesday. What started as an ambitious endeavor is starting to look like a legitimate newspaper, we hope, if a little more aesthetically radical. Like the movement itself, those of us producing the paper have had our ups and downs. We've had three changes of premises, two changes in format, and one arrest. Is it like this at *The Guardian*?

The range and quality of content has often exceeded our expectations. We perpetually drift between the surprised realization that another issue has been printed and the perplexed uncertainty whether next week's paper will live up to the standard. Some of our stories have been picked up by other publications (such as a news feature that analyzed the links of St. Paul's board of trustees to the financial industry), while other articles have led to discussions at Tent City University. Most articles have simply told stories, raised issues, and informed and educated our readers. In producing the newspaper, we have maybe become its foremost beneficiaries. Every one of us has undergone a process of political education and self-reflection.

In many ways, the newspaper appears to us as a microcosm of the camp. There are points of tension and disappointment. We are constantly confronted with the challenge of remaining open to new faces and fresh ideas despite our newly found structures. And we still have to ask ourselves the questions we have been asking for the past month. The answers we are able to provide next week or next month might be very different. As long as change remains an unfulfilled promise and the tents remain on the street, we will be here as well, writing, editing, publishing, and giving a voice to the many voices of this movement.

COUNTER-CASE STUDY

IRELAND FAILS TO RESPOND
TO ITS DEBT CRISIS

Andy Storey

Andy Storey is a lecturer in development studies at the School of Politics and International Relations, University College Dublin, and chairperson of the NGO Action from Ireland (Afri), which has carried out extensive advocacy and campaign work on debt and austerity in the Global South and in Ireland.

The Irish economy grew very rapidly from the mid-1990s onwards, earning the country the nickname "the Celtic Tiger." This growth was first based on the attraction of mainly U.S. multinationals availing themselves of a low corporate profits tax rate and, from the early 2000s, on a property price bubble that saw the economy become ever more dependent on the construction of overpriced and unnecessary buildings. The bubble burst in 2008, leaving the Irish banks effectively bankrupt and unable to service the debts they had accumulated from foreign financial institutions. The Irish state stepped in to guarantee those debts and has since slashed spending and raised taxes in order to do so. Thus, private debts have been taken into public ownership with disastrous social and economic consequences for the Irish.

Why were the Irish people not out on the streets in large numbers like their counterparts across Europe in 2011? Why did the Celtic dog never bark? It was not for the want of cause—the economic injustices being foisted on the Irish people were stark and onerous. Nor did people lack access to information on the nature of this injustice—a debt audit had laid bare the iniquitous nature of the Irish debt burden, and crippling austerity measures imposed by the Irish government were all in aid of paying off the bondholders owed by private Irish banks. But the bookkeeping was incredibly opaque, and to this day we have no idea who these bondholders are. The reaction, or lack thereof, to this glaring injustice was as baffling to me as it was frustrating. I was personally involved in uncovering this injustice through an audit of the Irish debt, which I will explain in more detail. We got the idea of doing an audit from Ecuador and other countries in the Global South where citizens had taken the initiative in untangling the web of secrecy and exploitation that had condemned them to debt servitude. I am a researcher and teacher in development studies and chairperson of a global justice NGO, so I was aware of these examples and keen to apply them to Ireland's newfound status as a victim of debt and austerity. But there seemed little interest amongst the wider society, or even among some other global development practitioners, in what these examples might teach us.

BAILING OUT THE BANKS: AT WHAT COST?

When the global financial crisis hit, asset values tumbled, leaving banks (including the Irish ones) in a parlous position. The Irish banks had borrowed heavily from abroad in the 2000s to lend onto their customers, mainly for investment in ever more expensive property. The Irish government chose to respond to the plight of the banks in an extraordinary manner: on September 30, 2008, all depositors and senior bondholders (creditors to the Irish banks) were guaranteed by the state. As historian Conor McCabe put it,

"The Irish people woke up to find that the . . . government had put up the entire Irish State as collateral for the crushing liabilities of six private banks." The total cost of bailing out the banks is so far estimated to be €70 billion and rising.

The price of all this is being paid by ordinary citizens: we have already witnessed more than €20 billion in "fiscal adjustment" in the form of spending cuts and tax increases, what economist Karl Whelan describes as "the equivalent of . . . €4,600 per person... the largest budgetary adjustments seen anywhere in the advanced economic world in modern times." As I write this, it's clear that 2011 will see €6 billion more of cuts and tax hikes, with further adjustments of between €3 billion and €4 billion for each year between 2012 and 2015.

A loan from the IMF and European Union was contracted in December 2010 as Ireland could no longer borrow at affordable rates from private financial markets. It is crucial to note that this is not a "bailout" of Ireland. The European Union and IMF intervened to ensure that Ireland would continue to pay back the money Irish banks owed to foreign financial institutions, with the bulk of the EU–IMF money merely routed through Ireland for that purpose. The conditions attached to this loan stipulate that austerity measures must be continued.

The social consequences are catastrophic, not least because the austerity policies are sending the economy into a tailspin. National income is already down over 15 percent from its peak level. Unemployment stands at almost 15 percent, close to half a million people. Emigration is estimated to be running at forty thousand per annum. The economy is mired in recession, with investment down from over €48 billion in each of 2006 and 2007, to a little over €18 billion in 2010. Bank loan approval rates fell from 95 percent in 2007 to 55 percent in 2010, and Ireland is now rated the second-lowest-ranking country in the European Union for provision of finance to small and medium-sized enterprises. Meanwhile, Irish banks, despite their newly cautious lending practices, are highly dependent on short-term loans of over €150 billion from the European Central Bank (ECB) and the Irish Central Bank.

LEARNING FROM THE GLOBAL SOUTH

What is happening in Ireland is not unique. Similar pain is being imposed on Greece, Portugal, and many other countries in Europe. But the record of such pain stretches well beyond the current era and well beyond Europe. For many years, Irish NGOs have highlighted issues surrounding Global South debt and IMF/World Bank structural adjustment, issues such as the erosion of sovereignty and the devastating socioeconomic consequences. As mentioned, I am the chairperson of a small global justice NGO—Action from Ireland (Afri)—and when the IMF arrived in Ireland in late 2010, it seemed obvious to me, and to some of my colleagues, that we were well placed to provide some analysis and critiques of the IMF (and EU) programme. This seemed to be especially the case given the striking parallels between some of the most controversial IMF operations in the Global South and the intervention in Ireland.

Specifically, Ajai Chopra, the head of the IMF team negotiating the Irish "bailout," previously worked in the IMF's Asia–Pacific department and led its rescue mission to South Korea after a financial collapse in 1997. In Korea, state interventions were curtailed and the government budget was slashed, despite the fact that government overspending had nothing to do with the Korean crisis. These actions lead to massive redundancies. Between 1996 and 1999, South Korea's unemployment rate tripled, and the proportion of the population identifying themselves as middle-class fell from 64 percent to 38 percent. Korean trade unions and other forces, including two candidates for presidential election, opposed these policies, but they were quickly assured that their opposition would count for nothing, as documented by Naomi Klein: "The

IMF refused to release the money until it had commitments from all four main candidates that they would stick to the new [IMF] rules if they won. With the country effectively held at ransom, the IMF was triumphant: each candidate pledged his support in writing."

Those development organisations that have long been monitoring such situations in Korea and elsewhere should have been best placed to help Irish people understand what was now happening to them. Instead, at a private meeting on the issue that I attended, a representative of an Irish development NGO announced, "I don't think the IMF in Ireland is the same as the IMF in developing countries." It was a shocking statement, reflecting a complete failure to understand that the same forces that had devastated the Global South could turn just as easily on Western nations. This failure ran the risk of missing an extraordinary opportunity to learn from how countries of the Global South had developed innovative strategies of resistance to economic austerity. The way democratically organised projects of popular power forced the Argentinian government to default on part of its debt in the early 2000s could have proven highly instructive for Irish people, for example, and development NGOs should have been perfectly placed to educate the Irish population on the parallels and possibilities to be drawn from the experiences in Argentina and elsewhere.

Similar lessons could have been drawn from debt audits, which have been used across the Global South to allow civil society to hold to account those responsible for the damage caused by their countries' indebtedness. Ecuador provides a particularly striking case. In 2007, President Rafael Correa established a debt audit commission, which reported in 2008 that a portion of the country's debt was indeed illegitimate and had done "incalculable damage" to Ecuador's people and environment. The price of illegitimate debt subsequently collapsed in the open markets, and Ecuador got rid of it easily. Despite predictions of economic disaster, the country registered 3.7 percent economic growth in 2010, and in 2011 the forecast for growth was in excess of 5 percent. The salience of this example for public debates in Ireland was glaringly obvious. Therefore, Afri, along with another NGO—the Debt and Development Coalition Ireland (DDCI)—and a trade union—Unite—commissioned three academic specialists in accountancy, economics, and finance to audit Ireland's debt, and their report was produced in September 2011. We deliberately decided that this would be a technical exercise, a fact-finding mission that would be all the more powerful for simply reporting the information in a neutral, dispassionate manner. Thus, while I and my colleagues sponsored the audit we carefully avoided any editorial interference. We wanted the results to speak for themselves, and indeed they made for startling reading.

THE SCALE AND SECRETIVE NATURE OF THE DEBT

The audit found that the Irish national debt stood at €371.1 billion on March 31, 2011. This was equivalent to almost 300 percent of Irish national income. Of this, €279.3 billion (over 75 percent) was accounted for by the state-covered debts of the Irish banks, and this, as the audit notes, was before taking into account the likelihood that much of the *direct* government debt may itself have arisen from the banking crisis. In other words, the audit proved conclusively that the Irish debt crisis was a crisis of *private*, and subsequently socialized, debt, not *public* debt. The allegedly "bloated" nature of the Irish public service, or "generous" welfare entitlements, did not cause this crisis, no more than they did in Korea.

Alarmingly, the headline audit figure of €371.1 billion may even have been an underestimate. It did not count unguaranteed bonds issued by the banks as part of the debt, for example. Legally, these bonds were not the responsibility of the Irish state, and yet the Irish government, presumably at the ECB's insistence, had been repaying these bonds also. In early November 2011, the government repaid in full an unguaranteed debt of $1 billion (approximately €731 million), which was owed by a now defunct bank to an unknown creditor—a debt which had previously been traded on the secondary market for little over half of its value. And, as I write, the Irish government seems insistent that it will not seek any debt relief despite the fact that such relief has been extended to Greece.

So who then was getting all this money? Another hugely important finding concerns secrecy, what the audit describes as "the anonymous nature of bonds, and the culture of confidentiality and secrecy which surrounds them." We simply *did not know* to whom the debt was owed and to whom it was being repaid, although we have strong suspicions. The fact that the ECB is opposing any debt write-down is compelling circumstantial evidence that the interests of major European financial institutions are at stake. The bondholders were obviously exerting enormous influence, directly or indirectly, over Irish government policy. Any attempt to ensure that the bondholders "took a haircut," or accepted some write-down in the value of the debt, was being strenuously resisted by the ECB in particular.

At the end of the day, this money probably cannot be repaid in full, and a default is likely. But the ECB and other dominant actors were explicitly demanding that the bondholders be paid off to the greatest extent possible, and that as much as possible of the debt be transferred to public ownership in advance of any possible default. This socialisation of bank losses was the simple logic of what was happening in Ireland (and in Greece and Portugal, and probably soon in other countries also). In the meantime, the Irish people have been asked to repay a debt that was not of their making and from which they gained little or nothing. This constitutes a *prima facie* case of illegitimate debt. And the lack of transparency meant that faceless market actors were exercising enormous influence over Irish government policy, which violated fundamental democratic principles that power should be exercised in an open and accountable manner.

THE UNDERLYING (ILLEGITIMATE AND UNDEMOCRATIC) AGENDA AND THE NEED FOR RESISTANCE

As if this were not bad enough, the Irish government was also using the excuse of the crisis to drive through other policies that likewise benefitted the corporate sector, such as reducing rates of pay for already low-paid workers despite the fact that a lack of wage competitiveness was not at the root of Irish problems. Between 2009 and 2010, wages and salaries declined from €37.3 billion to €34.9 billion, while profits of nonfinancial corporations increased from €35.2 billion to €37.8 billion. These gains were not translated into any increased economic activity as investment continued to fall. This is a classic example of what Naomi Klein calls the "shock doctrine" effect, whereby a crisis is used to ram through policies that restructure societies to the benefit of corporate interests. The same happened at the EU level, where the crisis was invoked to justify tighter surveillance of member-state budgets by the neoliberal EU Commission, with a view to further institutionalising austerity.

CAUSING THE CRISIS

Before coming to a conclusion, we must go back in time to see how we got to this place. Before the recent crash, Irish economic growth was, as mentioned, based largely on a property price bubble. By the end of 2011, house prices, which quadrupled between 1996 and 2007, were down 43 percent from their peak levels and probably had further to fall. Vast numbers of houses lay empty. What was fuelling the property price bubble was a massive rise in household debt, which shot upwards from €57 billion in 2003 to €157 billion in 2008. It was this trend that caused the last Irish minister for finance to claim that "we all partied." While it is certainly true that many people did borrow increasingly heavily during the boom, the actual *benefit*, if any, most people accrued from this is far from clear. Irish financial institutions increased their lending by 466 percent between 1998 and 2007—almost entirely to the

real estate and financial sectors rather than to the genuinely productive economy, with infrastructural investment in areas such as
transport, health, education, and telecommunications largely neglected. And the Irish banks were themselves borrowing in order
to lend on to their customers—the six main Irish banks borrowed
€15 billion from abroad in 2003. This figure had risen to €100 billion by 2007.

This reckless splurge was enabled by liberalised lending practices across the European Union, and by lax cross-border regulation of the financial sector. The low interest rate policy of the ECB
fanned the flames: the ECB variable rate was cut from 4.25 percent
in August 2001 to 2 percent in June 2003. Indeed, the very design of the Economic and Monetary Union (EMU) helped cause
the crisis by establishing exchange rates that left peripheral EU
countries uncompetitive relative to Germany and encouraged these
peripherals to rely on the accumulation of debt to compensate for
this. The Irish authorities also contributed to the property bubble
with a range of tax incentives for property development. And today
the Irish people are paying the heavy price in the form of foreclosed
homes, massive job losses, reduced social services, rising taxes, and
general economic despair.

SO WHAT'S NEXT?

In a nutshell, banks and property speculators, who caused the crisis, are getting bailed out by ordinary citizens. In the face then
of this appalling and glaring injustice, what are the Irish people
doing? Sadly, as mentioned at the outset, not enough. There have
been well-attended protest marches, but in 2010, only 511 Irish
workers were involved in industrial disputes. The audit did not
spark a mass popular protest, though we continue to work to popu-
larise and build on its findings, including launching a campaign to
expose the illegitimacy of the debts (being paid by the state) of one
particularly reckless and corrupt bank.

Why the relative inaction? There are several answers to this question. Many people did borrow recklessly during the boom years, so a certain sense of guilt may be at work, in at least some cases. People I know personally feel a certain unease that they bought in to the mania by buying second homes or unnecessary luxuries. And emigration acts as a safety valve, draining off potential social unrest. The mainstream media insists that there is no viable alternative to austerity and debt repayment, and, predictably, the audit report received limited media coverage. Furthermore, people invested huge hope in the election of February 2011, believing that a change of government would lead to a change of policies, as promised by the opposition parties. But instead, the same programme of austerity and bank bailouts continued. And then there was the largely nonconfrontational attitude of most trade union and civil society leaders, who sought to maintain a cooperative relationship with government and were loath to engage in militant protest.

But all is not doom and gloom. The 2011 election did not deliver the policy change the electors anticipated, but it did deliver the election of a sizeable number of members of parliament—some 20 percent of the total—both organised into parties and independents, who are firmly opposed to debt and austerity policies. There are also various citizens' initiatives emerging, including local "burn the bondholders" protests and, inspired by similar movements in Spain, the United States, and elsewhere, a citizens' occupation of the area around the Irish Central Bank. A coalition of groups is calling for a referendum on the debt with a view, on the part of some of the participants, at least, to its repudiation. We may not yet have seen Irish people take to the streets in large numbers as in Greece and Spain, but the anger is growing and, hopefully, the appetite for action. The Celtic dog may yet start barking.

AFTERWORD

SOCIAL MEDIA AND THE PROTESTS

Laurie Penny

Laurie Penny is a British blogger who writes under the name of Penny Red. She spends time in New York and London and writes for the New Statesman *and* The Nation. *This piece is adapted from the October 31, 2011, edition of* The Nation.

Over a year of protests, strikes, occupations, and anti-austerity uprisings across the Middle East, Europe, and now America, one thing has become clear: the changing nature of technology is changing the way that ordinary people think, act, and organise politically. This is happening in ways that world governments are, as yet, unable properly to anticipate or control. This, of course, does not mean that they are not trying.

The idea of the Occupy movement—of reclaiming physical and psychic territory at the heart of major cities and world finance centres in the name of social justice—was an idea whose time had come. It spread memetically, like a virus. The infectiousness of the idea relied on digital technology before and during its gathering of pace and profile, to organise the call-outs, to run live streams, Twitter feeds, and video clips that made millions of people across the world feel part of what was happening in Zuccotti Park, and to draw international attention to police brutality in the early days of the occupations without, crucially, any need to wait for the mediation of the mainstream press.

The organised, dedicated people gathering around the new networks of dissent and popular protest radiating from Occupy Wall Street are largely young, time-rich and digitally enabled—and unlike previous generations of protesters, they are able to create and disseminate their own media and control their own messaging. The story of technology and dissent in the modern protest movement, however, does not begin with Zuccotti Park. It begins in quiet bedrooms and obscure chat rooms tucked away in secret corners of the Internet, and its key protagonists make the most unlikely of heroes.

On a hot June morning in 2011 London's Westminster Magistrates' court, the kid in the dock could be auditioning for a starring role in the global psychodrama *The Little Guy Versus the State*. Pale, thin, and dwarfed by two enormous security guards, Jake Davis speaks in a whisper, and only to confirm his name. He is eighteen, from the remote Scottish archipelago of Shetland, and he is accused of being a key agent in an international cyberactivist collective called LulzSec, which has attacked the Web operations of entities ranging from the CIA to the Murdoch media empire. Davis is being charged with five computer-related offenses, including an attack on a major British police Web site and three counts of conspiracy. He seems to shrink inside his checked shirt, clutching a paperback titled *Free Radicals: The Secret Anarchy of Science*.

Hackers come in many forms, from criminals stealing credit card information to shadowy government organizations attacking enemy nuclear facilities; but today the most prominent and controversial are cyberactivists—or *hacktivists*, as Davis is alleged to be. Loosely affiliated and rapidly expanding, these groups have thousands of members all over the world and names like AntiSec (which stands for *anti-security*) and, most famously, Anonymous. These groups represent a new front in what has been labeled the "global information war": the growing battle over who controls information in cyberspace.

Operating anonymously, mainly via Internet relay chat (IRC) channels, hacktivist groups crash Web sites, hack servers, and steal passwords. Their signature move is the DDoS (distributed denial of service) attack, which involves coordinating thousands of computers to send traffic to a Web site until it overloads, crashes, and shuts down—the digital equivalent of a sit-in, except that coordinating a sit-in does not usually earn you ten years' jail time, which is what Davis faces if found guilty.

Hackers have traditionally been chat room pranksters; one of the accusations against Davis is his alleged role in hacking the *Sun*'s homepage, redirecting readers to a fake news story telling the world Rupert Murdoch was dead. There are snickers from the press bench as the prosecution reads the charge, and Davis finds it impossible to stop the littlest of grins from creeping across his face. For cyberactivists, it has always been about poking fun: an anarchic collision of satire and direct action that makes a mockery of the powerful and self-satisfied. They do it "for the lulz," in cyberspeak.

Over the past year, the work of these groups has become increasingly linked with a more serious mission, one that combats censorship on the Internet, whether by companies or governments. Anonymous in particular has become a powerful collective. At the Occupy Wall Street protests in New York, which Anonymous helped promote, young people wandered through the crowd in plastic Guy Fawkes masks—a symbol of collective, innominate popular resistance from the film and graphic novel *V for Vendetta*, which has been adopted by the group. In support of the protests, which target corporate greed and economic inequality, Anonymous posted a video online threatening to erase the New York Stock Exchange "from the Internet." Elsewhere in Liberty Plaza, young tech activists gave lectures on digital freedom and uploaded open-source software free of charge for anyone who'd brought along a laptop. Technology plays an essential role in the new networked people's movements that are springing up all over Europe, America, and the Middle East—and those movements have brought cyberactivism into its own. The generation that was supposed to have been made listless and apathetic by technology—the kids who were supposedly staring vacantly into virtual worlds in lonely bedrooms—are instead using technology to re-engage with current events in an era when the very principles of power are being rewritten on terms not wholly in the control of nation-states.

"There's not a whole lot of historical precedent" for cyberactivism on this scale, says Gabriella Coleman, who lectures on technology and anthropology at New York University. "It's hard to say what's going to happen, except that states are going to clamp down quickly."

Most security experts agree that sophisticated cyberattacks by nation-states, like the Stuxnet attack on an Iranian nuclear facility in 2010, are a far greater threat to global security than autonomous hacking collectives knocking out company Web sites. The former is the digital equivalent of state espionage; the latter, the equivalent of a road blockade or banner drop. Nonetheless, the FBI and other law enforcement bodies are concentrating a great deal of effort on these cyberprotesters. The United States has spent the past year recruiting hundreds of "white hat" hackers to fight cyberactivism and e-crime and has launched a global manhunt for members of Anonymous, LulzSec and other groups. It's also leaning on other countries to take similar measures: under U.S. pressure, Japan is considering requiring companies to share information about hackers with the government.

As the attacks have become more political—with more law enforcement agencies and major companies becoming targets of protest hacks—so has the backlash. Since this past summer, many suspected members of Anonymous, LulzSec, and other groups, some of them as young as sixteen, have been arrested in Europe and North America in a series of sting operations. Yet the attacks have continued, targeting, among others, more than seventy police

Web sites across the United States and the Syrian ministry of defense Web site, where the group posted a message of solidarity with the Syrian people. The iron-fisted response to relatively benign cyberactivism seems only to breed more of the same while diverting resources that could be used to pursue the type of cybercrime that actually poses a public threat.

Like so much on the Internet, in a way, contemporary hacktivism started with porn. Anonymous, for example, originated in the chat site 4chan, whose message boards are scurrilous back-channels full of filthy in-jokes.

Early DDoS attacks, starting in February 2010, targeted Australian authorities who tried to censor the distribution of cyberporn—a project code-named Operation Titstorm—as well as a proxy company that attempted to bring down The Pirate Bay, a file-sharing site for downloading music and videos. At stake was not so much nude photos or free MP3s but the very principle of free information exchange. In this sense, the trajectory of hacktivism from defending free file sharing to defending freedom itself may have been inevitable. "It started off with exposing titty videos to their friends," explains one member of the militant "tech dissent" collective DSG (Deterritorial Support Group), who identifies as Zardoz. "It ended with bringing down [an] autocratic regime."

He (or she) is referring to the Egyptian revolution, a key moment of politicization for cyberactivists, who stepped in to help the rebels with communications after Hosni Mubarak shut down the Internet. As the Arab Spring and subsequent global upheaval of the summer demonstrated, the fight for freedom of speech and action online has become enmeshed with the offline struggle for freedom of movement and thought. The "politicization of 4chan," as this trajectory is partially known among hacktivists, can be traced to WikiLeaks. After the whistle-blowing Web site released thousands of classified documents and diplomatic cables last fall, MasterCard and PayPal announced they would suspend payments to WikiLeaks, prompting members of Anonymous to shut down the companies' Web sites. Titled Operation Payback, the project changed the rules of engagement for those cyberactivists who had previously seen their anticensorship activities as separate from geopolitics. In this sense, WikiLeaks's great triumph has been to make the world think again about whether governments should have the right to withhold information from citizens and obstruct the free exchange of ideas online.

For young people around the world who grew up with the Internet—"digital natives"—the question is both profound and profoundly uncomplicated. Defending the freedom to share information online is more important than individual politics or morality. "That's why Anonymous intervened in WikiLeaks," explains Zardoz. "That's why they intervened in Tunisia. And that's why they intervened in Egypt." In Operation Egypt and Operation Tunisia, Anonymous and other groups coordinated to restore citizens' access to Web sites blocked by the government. The efforts extended beyond the Internet, with faxes used to communicate vital information as a means of last resort. (In classic "lulzy" style, cyberactivists also caused havoc by ordering enormous quantities of pizza delivered to Egyptian and Tunisian embassies.)

After Egypt, it became clear that the fight against censorship and the fight against state oppression were moving closer together. "This is not a minor struggle between state nerds and rogue geeks," wrote members of the DSG collective in June, in an influential blog post titled "Twenty reasons why it's kicking off in cyberspace." "This is the battlefield of the 21st century, with the terms and conditions of war being configured before our very eyes."

On this point, hacktivists and security experts agree. "LulzSec and Anonymous are exposing the huge number of vulnerabilities that are out there waiting to be exploited by someone who has the skills and the motivation," says Chris Wysopal, co-founder of Veracode, a security company based in Massachusetts. "Data is so leaky," says NYU's Coleman, "and if all you need to crack a government facility is a USB stick, can we really stop that happening?"

That's precisely the question that has state powers running scared. In these unsteady times, one of the few things we can know with any certainty is that the future is digital; the Internet—and the possibilities for collective engagement and disruption it offers—is not going away. It would take a massive worldwide program of censorship and surveillance both on- and offline to crack down on this, and that's just what "tech dissidents" are hoping to prevent.

The link between dissent by technology and dissent in the streets is growing stronger. The fact that ordinary citizens can get and share information instantaneously not only provides them with the tools to resist authority and evade arrest; it also delegitimizes that authority on practical and philosophical levels. Controlling information, after all, is one of the most important ways a state wields its power. Over nineteen months that have seen the nature and structure of power called into question around the globe, the nature and structure of technological dissent have grown and matured in kind. To police, the press, and the powerful, this evolving link between technology and dissent is cause for alarm: nobody knows what cyberactivists might be capable of next.

The crackdown on online dissent is part of the same trajectory of repression as the physical police brutality against Occupy movements and student protesters in Europe, America, and further afield. Online and offline dissent feed off and change one another, and one of the key ways in which they do so is in their attitude to the notion of "security" and what it means. The term has been a watchword for the generation that has grown up politically in a post-9/11 age, when world governments set out to ensure public complicity by promoting a form of modern statecraft whose role is first and foremost to provide "security"—in the sense of protection for the individual against shadowy alien enemies, rather than the sense of providing a basic level of social stability for the vulnerable and unfortunate. The questions that young people in particular have begun to ask—what is security for, who gets to police it, and just how many rights are we prepared to risk for it—are thrown into sharp relief in the online world, where the idea of security is inextricable from the idea of censorship. In cyberspace, freedom and security are usually in direct conflict. In a world where American police now routinely beat unarmed protesters bloody and torture them with chemicals whilst telling them that it's for their own safety, the question of how many freedoms ordinary people are prepared to forgo for the pitiless security offered by the Western governments is one which is beginning to receive a resounding answer.

Ultimately, one person's cyberterrorist is another person's digital freedom fighter, and for many, that's precisely what hacktivists are. In Liberty Plaza in October, the nerve center of the Occupy Wall Street protest was a makeshift media tent full of serious young people fussing over laptops in tangles of cables. Not all cyberactivists are young—stereotyping hacktivists as adolescent recluses is an easy way to dismiss their ideas—but there's one thing that teenagers and technologies can do far faster than grown-ups and governments, and that's adapt.

NOTES

1. Joseph E. Stiglitz, "Of the 1%, by the 1%, for the 1%," *Vanity Fair*, May 2011. http://www.vanityfair.com/society/features/2011/05/top-one-percent-201105.

2. See the research of Thomas Piketty and Emmanuel Saez, available at http://www.econ.berkeley.edu/~saez/ (accessed December 3, 2011) on income distribution. The share of wealth refers to net worth minus the value of one's home (i.e. "non-home wealth"). When home values are included, the top 1 percent of the population controls about 35 percent of the wealth. See http://www.levyinstitute.org/pubs/wp_589.pdf for both figures and http://www.federalreserve.gov/pubs/oss/oss2/papers/CDC.final.pdf for net worth figures.

3. The Gini coefficient is the indicator most commonly used to gauge income inequality in the world. Though flawed, it is useful for identifying broad trends. A perusal of the data compiled by the United Nations Development Programme shows the global trend of increasing inequality. See http://hdrstats.undp.org/en/indicators/67106.html. The World Top Incomes Database takes a different approach to analyzing inequality, using income tax records to track the proportion of national incomes held by top percentiles. These data also illustrate the trend. Of course, there are exceptions. Latin America, historically a region with some of the most unequal income distributions, has shown improvement in some countries. Argentina and Venezuela are two. Brazil still suffers from extreme inequality but has been improving in recent years.

4. According to the International Labour Organization. See

http://www.ilo.org/global/about-the-ilo/press-and-media-centre/news /WCMS_164543/lang--en/index.htm (accessed December 3, 2011).

5. As of August 2011, for 16–24-year-olds. See Bureau of Labor Statistics Web site, http://www.bls.gov/news.release/youth.nr0.htm (accessed December 3, 2011).

6. Using different definitions of what makes a "top school," various studies have provided telling numbers about the lack of economic diversity in elite universities. Research by Anthony P. Carnevale and Stephen J. Rose, cited by the Economic Policy Institute, showed earlier in the last decade that some 74 percent of top-school freshmen hailed from first-quartile families, while only 6 and 3 percent were from the bottom third and fourth quartiles, respectively. (Web site of the Economic Policy Institute, http://stateofworkingamerica.org/charts/income -quartile-of-the-entering-class-at-top-universities-and-community -colleges/, accessed December 29, 2011.) Other studies support this trend. See, for instance, Alexander Astin and Leticia Osequera, 2004, "The Declining 'Equity' of Higher Education," *Review of Higher Education*, 27(3):321–341.

7. In a *New York Times* poll on October 25, 2011, some two-thirds of respondents said that households earning a million dollars or more should face higher taxes. See http://www.nytimes.com/interactive /2011/10/26/us/politics/20111026_POLL.html?ref=politics (accessed December 3, 2011).

8. See *USA Today*, http://www.usatoday.com/news/nation /story/2011-10-17/poll-wall-street-protests/50804978/1.

9. Reported in the media. See, for instance, http://www.dailymail .co.uk/news/article-2048754/Occupy-Wall-Street-Bloomberg-backs -dawn-eviction.html (accessed December 3, 2011).

10. Susan S. Silbey, "Rotting Apples or a Rotten Barrel," http://www .nae.edu/File.aspx?id=10416.

11. In the nineteenth century, these ideas were referred to as *social Darwinism*. A variant concept was popularized among the right, but the intellectual underpinnings are weak. See also Stiglitz (1994).

12. All government employees were given an RCD card for free, which helped Ben Ali inflate the party membership in Tunisia.

13. It still feels remarkable to be able to publicly name a co-conspirator this way, something that would be a deadly betrayal in the time before the revolution. Achraf Aouadi was an inspiration for me, and founded the watchdog organization I Watch, over which I now

preside. He is currently a master's student studying English literature in Tunis.

14. Al-Wefaq has a political Islamic agenda and represents mostly Shia voters.

15. The Haq Movement for Liberty and Democracy formerly had an overlapping agenda with Al-Wefaq. Haq has adopted a less engaged approach with the regime. In 2010 Bahraini authorities reportedly accused the group's leader of "leading sabotage cells."

16. Known as the Persian Gulf in the United States, the body of water between Iran and the Arabian Peninsula is called the Arabian Gulf in Arab countries. For clarity, the editors refer to it as "the Gulf" throughout the chapters on Bahrain.

17. See http://www.state.gov/secretary/rm/2010/12/152355.htm.

18. See http://www.hrw.org/sites/default/files/reports/bahrain0210 webwcover.pdf.

19. Amnesty International, "Bahrain Activists Must Receive a Fair Trial," September 6, 2010.

20. See http://files.bici.org.bh/BICIreportEN.pdf, page 465.

21. See http://files.bici.org.bh/BICIreportEN.pdf, point 1246.

22. See http://files.bici.org.bh/BICIreportEN.pdf, point 1722 (h).

23. In late November 2011, protests again erupted in Bahrain, before and after the BICI report was released.

24. See http://bahrainrights.hopto.org/en/node/4849.

25. See http://www.amnesty.org/en/library/asset/MDE11/009/2011 /ar/40d6fa8f-464f-416d-84c0-3ea391629a09/mde110092011en.pdf.

26. The towering, iconic monument in the middle of the Pearl Roundabout became a symbol of the uprising. It was demolished by authorities when the area was cleared of protesters.

27. "Uprising" in Arabic.

28. The secret police.

29. See the Al Jazeera documentary *Bahrain: Shouting in the Dark* at http://www.aljazeera.com/programmes/2011/08/201184144547798162. html.

30. See video at http://www.youtube.com/watch?v=X7vst991EEg &Ir=1.

31. See video at http://www.youtube.com/watch?v=xfodjooI6ys.

32. See video at http://www.youtube.com/watch?v=cx8SkQvSR38.

33. See video at http://www.youtube.com/watch?v=lyi6W8y2K0o.

34. See http://www.palmbeachpost.com/money/real-estate/deadbeat
-fights-back-against-foreclosure-process-981385.html.

35. See http://www.floridasupremecourt.org/pub_info/foreclosure
_comments.shtml and http://www.floridasupremecourt.org/pub_info
/summaries/briefs/09/09-1460/index.html, and the Florida Supreme
Court's response at http://www.floridasupremecourt.org/pub_info
/summaries/briefs/09/09-1460/index.html.

36. See http://4closurefraud.org/2011/02/20/comments-re-nj
-emergent-rule-amendments-the-art-of-the-dodge, and http://4closure
fraud.org/2011/01/10/letter-to-the-new-jersey-supreme-court
-concerning-fraudulant-documents-filed-in-foreclosure-proceedings
-w-exhibits.

37. See http://www.aclu.org/files/assets/2010-11-17-CanadyLetter
.pdf.

38. See Florida's 4th DCA original and revised opinions *Riggs v.
Aurora Loan Services, LLC* (4D08-4635) and *Glarum v. LaSalle* (4D10-
1372).

39. See http://articles.sun-sentinel.com/2011-03-07/news
/fl-foreclosure-david-stern-law-firm-c20110307_1_djsp-enterprises
-jeffrey-tew-foreclosure-cases, and http://blogs.palmbeachpost.com
/realtime/2011/04/28/ben-ezra-katz-to-close-second-south-florida
-foreclosure-firm-to-shut-its-doors, and http://dealbook.nytimes
.com/2011/11/21/foreclosure-firm-steven-j-baum-to-close-down.

40. See http://online.wsj.com/article/SB10001424052748703551304
576260952761726790.html.

41. See http://www.nytimes.com/2011/12/25/business/foreclosure
-relief-dont-hold-your-breath-fair-game.html?_r=1&ref=gretchenmor
genson.

42. See http://www.americanbanker.com/bankthink/Lippman
-Lawsky-Schneiderman-New-York-foreclosure-1044045-1.html.

43. See http://swampland.time.com/2011/05/09/foreclosure-probe
-chief-asked-bank-lawyers-for-money, and http://www.palmbeachpost
.com/news/state/early-on-florida-attorney-general-pam-bondi
-shows-1903187.html.

44. See http://www.palmbeachpost.com/money/foreclosures/former
-state-investigator-takes-job-at-foreclosure-firm-1718297.html.

45. See http://www.thefloridacurrent.com/article.cfm?id=25597745.